GOOD·OLD·DAYS®

BEST OF THE
GOOD OLD DAYS™

GARDEN

V

FOR VICTORY

Edited by Ken and Janice Tate

HOUSE of
WHITE
BIRCHES
PUBLISHERS
SINCE 1947

Best of the Good Old Days™

Editors: Ken and Janice Tate
Managing Editor: Barb Sprunger
Editorial Assistant: Joanne Neuenschwander
Copy Supervisor: Michelle Beck
Copy Editors: Läna Schurb, Judy Weatherford

Publishing Services Director: Brenda Gallmeyer
Art Director: Brad Snow
Assistant Art Director: Nick Pierce
Graphic Arts Supervisor: Ronda Bechinski
Graphic Artists: Nicole Gage, Janice Tate
Production Assistants: Marj Morgan, Jessica Tate, Judy Neuenschwander
Photography: Tammy Christian, Don Clark, Matthew Owen
Photo Stylist: Tammy Steiner

Chief Executive Officer: David McKee

Printed in the China
First Printing: 2008
Library of Congress Number: 2007933467
ISBN: 978-1-59217-202-3
Good Old Days Customer Service: (800) 829-5865

Every effort has been made to ensure the accuracy of the material in this book.
However, the publisher is not responsible for research errors or typographical mistakes in this publication.

Except where noted, all cover illustrations are courtesy
the House of White Birches nostalgia archives, DRG Publishing. All rights reserved.

We would like to thank the following for the art prints used in this book.
For fine-art prints and more information on the artists featured in *Best of the Good Old Days* contact:
Jim Daly, P.O. Box 25146, Eugene, OR 97402, www.jimdalyart.com
Wild Wings Inc., Lake City, MN 55041, (800) 445-4833, www.wildwings.com

1 2 3 4 5 6 7 8 9

Dear Friends of the Good Old Days,

Back in 1993, my dear wife Janice and I put together a special commemorative issue of *Good Old Days* magazine, celebrating our 30th year of publication. I said then that ours was one nostalgia magazine that could actually get nostalgic about itself.

Good Old Days is now closing on half a century of telling the stories of ordinary folks who have lived such extraordinary lives. Those stories have been told by the loyal readers of the magazine, people of every walk of life and of every ethnicity.

The magazine began as a column in *Women's Circle*, a magazine published by Edward Kutlowski and Tower Press. The column invited readers to share their stories, old-time songs and poetry, favorite recipes, etc. It wasn't long until Ed noted how quickly the popularity of the column had grown.

Ed was a pioneer in "niche" publishing, a concept still ahead of its time in the 1950s and early 1960s. He suspected that there might be a niche for a nostalgia magazine, so he pulled the column from *Women's Circle* and spun off *Good Old Days.* Time has borne witness that Ed was right. In the five decades since its birth, the magazine has grown into a publication with a readership of over 300,000.

I believe our readers have recognized that the magazine is a natural extension of the great American tradition of oral history. How many of us sat on grandparents' laps and listened to the countless telling and retelling of tales from the old days? I remember begging my Grandma Stamps to "tell me again"

the stories of life in Oklahoma before it was a state; of her father who ran a ferry on the Grand River when only horses and wagons crossed; of my great-grandmother, a beautiful Indian woman the family had to leave behind in a reservation graveyard.

I heard Grandma's stories so many times that I could almost recite them myself. "And then you and Great-Grandpa came back to Arkansas in a covered wagon, right?" I'm sure my adolescent prompting was good cause for Grandma to find more tolerable things to do—like cleaning the oven. But she didn't. She tolerated me and helped weave me into the fabric of our family's history.

Then, like a ribbon of heritage tying generation to generation, I recited those oft-told tales to my own children.

Grandma made her mark in the world by sharing her story. That is what the readers of *Good Old Days* have done. They have left their mark by telling their stories.

So, as Janice and I began planning our next *Good Old Days* book, we thought it would be appropriate to go back and pull some of the best stories from the first 40 years of the magazine. We have included the date of original publication for each story, and we have reproduced the cover of the magazine in which each story appeared.

We know you will enjoy this nostalgic look at "The Magazine That Remembers the Best." Join us as we remember the *Best of the Good Old Days.*

Ken Tate

❧ Contents ❧

In the Beginning • 6

The Memories Continue • 42

A New Home • 86

Looking Back • 124

GOOD OLD DAYS
A Monthly Magazine

The GOOD OLD DAYS with TED MILLER

MORE MOTORING MEMORIES

REMEMBER WHEN WE HAD **TWO** SPARES ON BACK?

AND DAD USED TO PUMP THEM UP BY HAND?

48791

FLAT TIRES WERE AN EXCUSE TO EXPLORE NEW TERRITORY—

IT WASN'T ALWAYS EASY TO BE ON TIME..

SOME OF THOSE OLD TIRES HAD THEIR GOOD POINTS—

—THOSE WERE THE SWINGIN' GOOD OLD DAYS!

The '60s:
In the Beginning

Chapter One

In 1964, when Edward Kutlowski began publication of *Good Old Days*, the first volume of the magazine was printed in a tabloid format. Ed and I first met in the 1980s, and after we became friendly enough for me to ask what he might consider a "fool question," I pressed him on why he produced the magazine in a newspaper style that first year.

"I knew I had a winner in *Good Old Days*," Ed replied, "and I didn't want anyone to steal the idea from me. I couldn't afford to print another magazine, so I registered the name and printed it as a tabloid until I could."

Ed didn't hold onto any of those old tabloids, so my wife and I began a systematic search for them that has continued for nearly 20 years. We have visited hundreds of flea markets and even browsed online to find seven copies. The earliest of the tabloids we found was September 1964; it was the seventh issue produced. (The cover of that treasured tabloid is reproduced at left.)

After the cover cartoon, the magazine contains a look back to etiquette in the late 19th century, early marriage customs in central Illinois, two pages of photographs of old-time homes and early "horseless carriages," several classic advertisements and a look at silent films from 1916.

There was also a column called "Wanted" where readers could request old favorite recipes, words to old songs or poems, and help in locating old friends and relatives. The "Wanted" column continues to be an important, popular feature in the magazine.

My wife and I are always amazed at how *Good Old Days* readers are willing to help other readers with their requests. It is a testimony to the kind of community the magazine has built through the decades.

As the editor and publisher, Ed wrote a column called "The Old-Timer" beginning with the July 1965 issue. (See page 9 for Ed's first column.) "The Old-Timer" became the standard for all of the editor columns that followed, even to my own popular "Looking Back" feature today.

Good Old Days was Ed's favorite magazine, he told me a year before his death in 2006 at age 91. He continued to edit the magazine for about 16 years, despite an increasingly busy schedule as president of House of White Birches and Tower Press. He held the honor of being editor for the longest term until I recently passed my 17th year as editor.

Ed also continued to be an avid reader of the magazine, even after he sold his publishing company in 1985. He was a friend, a mentor and an inspiration to me. All that *Good Old Days* has become must ultimately be laid at his feet. Even though he was a man of vision, he always looked forward to looking backward to the time we call the Good Old Days.

—Ken Tate

A Midnight Explosion

By D.E. Rawlings

In 1909, when I was a boy 11 years of age, my family and I spent six weeks visiting my grandmother in Sumner, Ill. We returned to Sumner in 1910 and remained there the greater part of the year.

My brother and I liked to go to the railroad depot and watch the Baltimore and Ohio's St. Louis-bound mail train scamper through town at 60 miles per hour. The outgoing mail was snapped from the bracket and the local mail was booted out the mail car door. When the heavy mail bags struck the ground, they bounced and rolled end over end for a considerable distance, like so many tumbleweeds. I heard that a man had been killed some previous year when he was struck by one of those hurtling mail bags.

At about midnight, a similar train headed from St. Louis to Washington would repeat the performance. However, my brother and I were not on hand at that hour to view the spectacle.

Jessie Skaggs was the town marshal. One night Jessie was at the depot when the midnight mail train came through. The uproar created by the speeding train was fading in the distance when Jessie heard a dull explosion coming from the business district.

The marshal decided to investigate. He was walking past the post office when he observed a light in front of the safe. In the light of a dark lantern, Jessie saw the dim outlines of two men. They had blown open the outer safe door and were working on the inner plate door when the marshal spotted them in the act.

(If the explosion had occurred while the train was speeding through town, it probably would not have been heard. This may have been a miscalculation on the burglars' part.)

Open warfare developed at once. The large window in front of the post office erupted in splinters of glass. The General Delivery boxes inside were punctured and shattered by flying bullets. But Jessie stood his ground, shooting it out with the burglars. Suddenly, one of the safecrackers dashed to a back window and disappeared in the alley. His partner followed just as Jessie fired one final shot. The man lurched against the windowsill, then crawled through the open window.

Later that morning, excitement ran high in the normally quiet little town as the grapevine came to life. Soon nearly the entire township knew about the attempted burglary. And Jessie became the hero of Sumner—a tribute he rightly deserved.

My brother and I were caught up in the excitement and were soon on the job. Boylike, we managed to keep well up in the front ranks. We saw the hounds arrive from a neighboring town. We saw the dogs pick up the scent—and the chase was on. The dogs led us on a chase around the business district, through part of the residential section, then back to the business district. There, in a blind alley, behind some crates and boxes, was found the body of one of the safecrackers. As far as I know, his partner was never apprehended.

The dead man was buried, apparently without identification, in the Sumner Cemetery.

MAY 1965

The GOOD OLD DAYS (WITH TED MULLER)

World's GREATEST MOVIES

TODAY A MILLION DOLLAR SPECTACULAR IN YOUR OWN LIVING ROOM IS APT TO BE A BORE, BUT —

REMEMBER THOSE MAGIC LANTERN SHOWS?

JUST A BED SHEET

THOSE WERE THE GOOD OLD DAYS!

My grandmother was Postmaster Culbertson's next-door neighbor. One day, Culbertson said he had received orders to exhume the body to obtain fingerprints. When the time arrived for the exhumation, Culbertson and another man—the coroner, I presume—set out afoot for the cemetery, which was but a short jaunt from town. My brother and I tagged along.

The grave was opened. Ever since that day, I have marveled at the fortitude and stamina of Culbertson and his co-worker as they attended to their sickening task. Owing to the advanced state of decomposition, fingerprinting was extremely difficult. But the prints were obtained.

Some time later, word was received that the dead man had been identified as Charles Mitchell, who had a police record around the East Coast. ❖

—Originally published in May 1965.

The Old-Timer

First Good Old Days *editorial by Edward Kutlowski*

Some folks say that the "Good Old Days" were rough and tough on muscles and nerves, with little or no comfort. Mebbe so sometimes, but there were many things in those days that we cannot duplicate now.

Every time I walk into a supermarket, I think of shopping back in the 1900s, 1920s and even the 1930s. Who will say that our shopping today is any more comfortable than in the old days?

You could walk into a big market in those days and march right up to a counter and be waited on like you were the most important thing that stepped into the store. If you weren't satisfied by what you saw in the showcase, then the clerk would go in the back room and try to please you. If you bought a dozen oranges, you could see each one as it went into the bag. No self-respecting clerk would throw in a rotten orange in the lot.

Today, oranges come already packed in a bag—and so does everything else in the fruit or vegetable line. No one can see completely what he has bought until he is home and torn open the package.

Time and again a particular spoiled vegetable or fruit will be in the package. True, they are not packed like that, but lying around in the warehouse and in the store will bring about this condition, and there is little anyone can do about it. I suppose you can squawk about it, but sometimes this is just too much work and effort—especially if the supermarket is miles and miles away.

Remember when every market had its own delivery system? You could call in your order and have it delivered to your home. Or if you made up the order in the store, you could have it delivered to your home. If you did business regularly at one place and were familiar with the manager, then you could be sure that your telephone order would receive careful attention.

Today, not one store in a hundred will deliver anything to your home. You must do all the work. You push the carriage up and down the aisles, then get into a line at the checkout counter, [and] lay out everything on the counter. The clerk hands you the filled bags and you have to haul it out to your car and from there to your home. It's haul, haul all the way. Self-service, phooey! It's another word for doing *all* the work and getting very little (if any) service from the store. Little wonder that there are supermarkets on almost every corner, and more coming up regularly!

What's wrong with walking to the store, handing the clerk your shopping list and then confining your activities to seeing what the clerk chooses to select for your order? The clerk picks out the order, packs it and then, if you want, delivers it to your home. *This was shopping a half century ago—even 30 years ago!*

What was wrong with this? I wish that I knew why folks say that supermarkets are a big step forward. I don't find them convenient, and there are many days when I think back to shopping in the Good Old Days and sincerely wish that they were *with us again!* ❖

—Originally published in July 1965.

Good Old School Days

By Mrs. Jean Bruening

A mong the many blessings that my life has claimed, I feel one of them was the privilege of attending a little one-room school. The older pupils recited their advanced studies in the same room that the younger children occupied, and I still cherish the memories of those fascinating recitations that I listened to, even though a lot of it passed over my head.

The older children on the playground made a comfortable background for the younger ones, and in many cases, they kept the game from getting too rough or unfair.

Very few pupils lived close enough to go home for lunch, and for those who stayed at school, that hour between 12 and 1 p.m. was the highlight of the day. In warm weather, the dinner buckets—most of them lard pails—were taken to a nice, shady place in the yard and the contents compared and sometimes traded. As the days grew colder, we'd gather 'round the big rectangular stove that stood near the center of the front of the schoolroom, and we'd have the "mostest" fun.

If the weather was cold, we played guessing games in the room.

Did you ever set a couple of black apple seeds on a hot stove and watch them pop? It was interesting to see which seed popped first. Great fun, especially if the seeds had been given a girl's name and a boy's name. If they popped toward each other, it was supposed to mean marriage; if away from each other, vice versa.

Or did you ever watch eagerly while the seeds in an apple core were counted to see if a certain boy loved you? There was such excitement if the number of seeds proved to be 12; the rhyme is as follows:

> *One, he loves; two, he loves;*
> *Three, he loves, they say.*
> *Four, he loves with all his heart,*
> *Five, he casts away.*
> *Six, he loves; Seven, he loves;*
> *Eight they both love.*
> *Nine, he comes; Ten, he tarries;*
> *Eleven, he woos; Twelve, he marries.*

What happy noon hours they were, with the friendly lady teacher looking on, smiling.

If the weather was cold, we played guessing games in the room. Most days, however, we played in the yard—such games as Steal

Sticks, Base Tag, Anti-High-Over and Run Sheep Run, though there weren't many places to hide in our yard.

When the teacher rang the bell, we all rushed to our special places in line—boys in one line, girls in the other. We had to march in quietly, and there was perfect silence while the roll was called. Then, while the teacher called the groups to the front of the room for class, the rest of us knew just where to look on the board for our assigned tasks.

If our work was done before the teacher was ready for our class, we would stand our geography books in front of us on the desk—two children sat in each seat—and from behind those geographies, little autograph books could be passed around without disturbing the discipline of the room. In them, friends wrote such verses as these:

Way back here, out of sight,
I'll write my name just for spite,
　　or,
　If you see a cat, climb a tree,
　Pull its tail and think of me.

I still treasure my album of such verses.

Happiest of all are my memories of our Christmas concerts. What a happy month December was, for we'd start to practice dialogues, recitations and songs for the annual event. What a delightful feeling it was to come out onto the stage, wearing long skirts like our mothers wore; and how we laughed when we saw the older boys wearing long pants and moustaches!

When the concert was over, there was a Christmas tree with presents and colored net bags of candy, nuts, and an orange for all—and Santa Claus to distribute them. What a thrill when we heard the sleigh bells announce his arrival!

Then there were refreshments for all and a dance for the older folks while we children sat on benches around the wall, watching. Needless to say, our eyes were mostly on the teacher as she danced the lancers, three-step or waltzed with the young country swains.

When evening ended, we'd all wend our various ways homeward, tired but happy, guided by the light from lanterns. What child could ever forget these memories! Now, more than 50 years later, they are still fondly remembered by one who, for eight years, attended and loved a little one-room school. ❖

　　　　　—Originally published in July 1965.

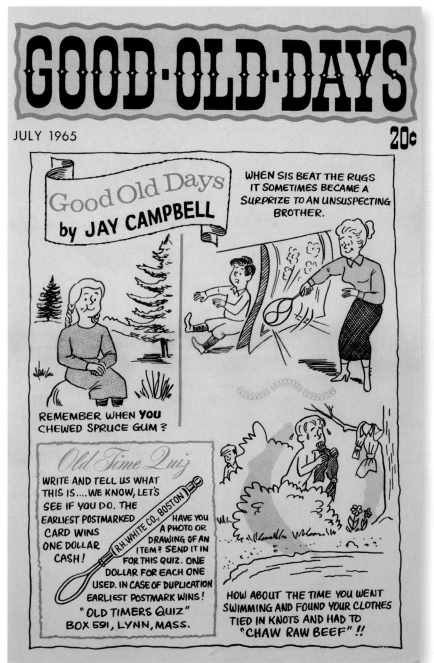

Memory Gems

By Margaret Ferguson

How happily I recall the last half-hour of the day in the fourth grade devoted to "memory gems." Perhaps I enjoyed it so because I was gifted with an excellent memory for rhyme and verse, and so I excelled in reciting these bits of wisdom. In June came Exhibition Day, when the schoolroom was decorated with pails of lilacs and wildflowers, the blackboards around the room were adorned by teacher with hand-drawn borders of fruits and flowers and leaves in colored chalk, and our favorite "memory gems" were written in beautiful Spencerian script. To the child who had helped to scrub and clean the blackboards in preparation for this grand event, the results were a joy to behold.

The parents and friends who were invited guests admired our decorations, too, but were more interested in hearing the children and applauding them as they answered questions, read compositions, recited verse and sang in chorus. Here are some of the "memory gems" that still impress me, though 50 years have now elapsed.

GOOD·OLD·DAYS

FEB. 1966   25¢

*When the Breton sailor puts
to sea, his prayer is, "Keep me, O
God, for my boat is so small and
Thy ocean is so wide."*

*For want of a nail the shoe was lost.
For want of a shoe the horse was lost.
For want of a horse the rider was lost.
For want of a rider the battle was lost.
For want of a battle the kingdom was lost.
And all for the want of a horseshoe nail.*

The moral of the first verse is man's dependence on the Almighty; and of the second, the importance of little and seemingly invaluable things in the scheme of living.

*Two little squirrels out in the sun;
One gathered nuts, the other had none:
"Time enough yet," was his constant refrain,
"Summer is still only just on the wane."*

*Listen, my child, while I tell you his fate.
He roused him at last,
but he roused him too late;*

Down fell the snow in a pitiless cloud,
And the starved little squirrel
was wrapped in a shroud.

Two little boys in a schoolroom were placed:
One always working, the other disgraced:
"Time enough yet for learning," he said;
"I will climb, by and by, from the foot to the head."

Listen, my children. Their locks turned gray:
One lives in comfort and honour today;
The other, a pauper, looks out at the door
Of the poorhouse, and idles his days as of yore.

Probably some small ears were spurred on
to study because of these wise words. No doubt,
many were quite deaf to the meaning of them.

But pleasures are like poppies spread;
You seize the flow'r, its bloom is shed;
Or like the snow falls on the river;
A moment white—then melts forever. ...
—from *Tam o' Shanter* by Robert Burns

Silently, one by one,
in the infinite meadows of heaven,
Blossomed the lovely stars,
the forget-me-nots of the angels.
—from *Evangeline* by H.W. Longfellow

The last verse, those beautiful words of
Henry Wadsworth Longfellow, became the
diamond among my gems when I grew up.
Whenever I walked under the stars on a clear
fall or winter night, they seemed so much
brighter and closer to me than usual.

The following made me more willing to
work in the garden—also, in the garden of life.

Oh! A wonderful thing is a seed;
The one thing deathless ever,
The one thing changeless, utterly true,
For ever old, forever new,
And fickle and faithless never.

Plant hate, and hate will spring;
Plant love, and love will grow;
Today you may sow, tomorrow will bring
The blossoms that show what sort of a thing
Is the seed, the seed that you sow.

A gloomy frown and a merry word
Went out for a walk one day;
And they spoke to all they chanced to meet—
The sick, the sad, and the gay.

The sick man smiled at the merry word,
And the sad one looked less sad,
And the gay one laughed till his jolly tune
Made all the echoes glad.

To the gloomy frown scarce a glance they gave,
But hurried to pass him by,
Afraid, if they looked at his face too long,
They'd echo his dismal sigh.

And ever it's so as we journey on
And meet them along the way;
We turn from the one with a shiver and sigh;
The merry word wins the day.
—Author Unknown

Speak gently, 'tis a little thing
Dropped in the heart's deep well;
The good, the joy, that it may bring,
Eternity shall tell.
—from *Speak Gently* by G.W. Langford

Some of us learned longer poems, which we
recited in competition for small prizes. I remember winning a nice, shiny-new Canadian 25-cent
piece, which I treasured for years. Among the
titles of the longer poems, I recall Longfellow's
The Children's Hour; *The Wreck of the Hespe-*
rus; some stanzas of *The Chambered Nautilus*;
and *St. Peter at the Golden Gate*.

When I was somewhat older, I memorized
the poems *Lasca*; *The Little Toy Dog*; and *Abou*
Ben Adhem. I also taught these to underprivi-
leged girls who wanted to take part in entertain-
ments but had no particular talent.

I hope you, readers, will recall the Good
Old Days when you, too, recited some of these
verses. And I hope that you will also relive the
feeling of the sheer beauty of the words of the
immortals, and the sense of accomplishment
you experienced when your recitation was over,
your shyness faded away, and the butterflies in
your innards gave way to hunger for the refreshments you knew awaited the victorious. ❖

—Originally published in February 1966.

Looking Hollywood Way

By Harry Wilkinson

hirley Temple! The mere mention of her name brings forth a flood of golden memories of the dimpled favorite of the '30's, whom many considered the greatest child star of all time. Many, many haven't forgotten—and don't want to forget—the hours of pleasure her screen appearances brought to them in the happy days before World War II, when her smile, her tapping, dancing feet and her songs entranced them.

Seems a long time back and hard to realize that Shirley, born April 23, 1928, in Santa Monica, this year will become 38 years of age—a happy wife and mother, Mrs. Charles Black, out on the West Coast. She was "America's Sweetheart" then, likened to the first "sweetheart" we recall so well, Mary Pickford, still living today at 73. Shirley's career started at age 3 in educational two-reel comedies, then *The Red-Haired Alibi* at 4, many fine films, and on to, I believe, her last film in 1949, *A Kiss for Corliss.*

After a 10-year retirement, she appeared on TV in the *Shirley Temple Story Book Hour,* later *The Shirley Temple Show,* as hostess and frequent star of a color series of children's classics. Throughout the years her old films have run and rerun on TV. Somewhere in the country on some channel today or tonight there will be a Temple oldie revived, and you can bet a happy audience will greet it.

It was my pleasure 30 years ago to plug for 20th Century Fox some 17 of the Temple pictures, and shout her good name from the housetops through the use of press books, an abundance of beautiful stills, and informal studio and at-home poses.

I'll list a few titles just to refresh your memory. There was *Bright Eyes* back in 1934; *The Littlest Rebel* with John Boles; *The Little Colonel* with Lionel Barrymore; *Captain January,* one of my favorites, with veterans Guy Kibbee and Slim Summerville in the cast; *Stowaway* with Alice Fay and Robert Young; *Dimples* with good old Frank Morgan; *Rebecca of Sunnybrook*

Above: Shirley Temple. Facing page, top: William Demarest with Shirley in *Rebecca of Sunnybrook Farm. Right:* Shirley as Sara with Ian Hunter as her father in *The Little Princess.*

Farm; the wonderful *Heidi*; *Wee Willie Winkie* with Victor McLaglen; *Little Princess* with Ian Hunter and Arthur Treacher; *Just Around the Corner*; *Little Miss Broadway* with dancing star George Murphy; *Blue Bird* with Spring Byington; *Susannah of the Mounties*; *Young People*

with Jack Oakie; and *Kathleen* would bring the date up to 1941.

Many of the fine character folk who starred with Shirley in her succession of films have long since departed from the film world—John Barrymore, Bill Robinson, Jean Hersholt, Slim Summerville, Guy Kibbee, and Frank Morgan, just to name a few who probably were delighted to work in a film with the clever youngster.

Needless to say, I prize the eight old stills that Shirley autographed for me back in 1963 from her Woodside, Calif., residence. Two in particular are most interesting, as they show her with beloved Carole Lombard and Gary Cooper from the 1943 *Now and Forever,* and another with her devoted mother and dad. ❖

—*Originally published in February 1966.*

Editor's note: *This "Looking Hollywood Way" was the first column by Harry Wilkinson published in* Good Old Days *magazine. Harry, who already had retired from a career as a Hollywood publicist, wrote for the magazine for 33 years until his death in 1999 at the age of 91.*

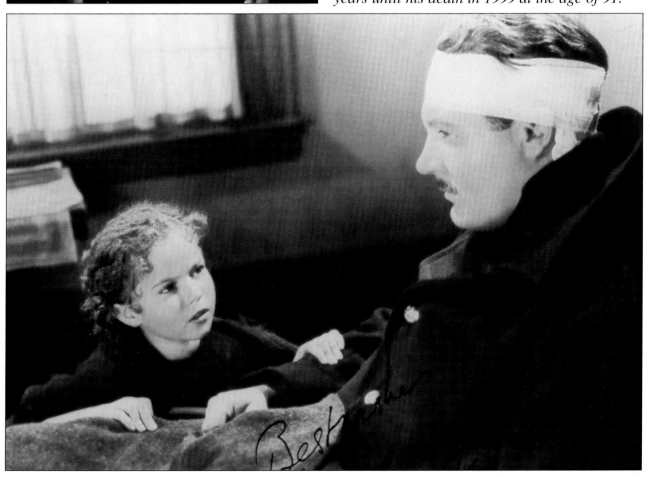

GOOD·OLD·DAYS

MAY 1966

25¢

I Remember the Jubilee

By Nellie Stringham

I wonder how many older folks ever attended a jubilee. In the community where I was raised, they were annual affairs. I was raised, along with five brothers and sisters, on a farm a few miles from the lovely little town of Lenora, Kansas, in the northwest part of the state. (This town has never grown much; it is still a "lovely little town.")

There were three big occasions each year: Christmas, July Fourth and the jubilee. The first two of those holidays were celebrated big, as they were every other place; but the jubilee was extra special, and we all looked forward to this occasion.

It was held in August each year and lasted two or three days, depending on the prosperity of the community. A carnival would be hired, and it would be set up on the main street of our little town— merry-go-round, Ferris wheel, side shows, booths to test one's ability at shooting, throwing, and so on. These little carnival companies seemed to have everything!

When the carnival filled the main part of town, it seemed so strange.

For me and some other children in the vicinity, Lenora was the only town we had ever seen. When the carnival filled the main part of it, it seemed so strange—as if we had traveled a long way to a new, foreign place.

We made many preparations on the farm for this occasion. Outside, Papa would see that fieldwork and chores were caught up so he could leave them.

Inside, there was much more excitement. Young chickens were caught and put in coops, ready to be killed and fried. Beets were pulled from the garden and pickled. There was baking to do—cookies, cakes, bread. Clothes had to be washed, starched stiff and ironed—an outfit for each day. We all washed our hair, and we children all bathed and scrubbed.

Then came the first big morning. We were all up at daylight. The cows were milked and turned into the pastures with the extra horses. Water and feed was put out for the hogs and chickens. The chickens we had penned up had to be killed and cooked while we ate breakfast.

Afterward, lunch baskets were filled; then everyone cleaned up.

Facing page: *Good Old Days* magazine cover, May 1966, House of White Birches nostalgia archives

Old Pete and Mabel were hitched to the wagon, and everything was loaded in.

Papa and Mama sat on the spring seat at the front of the wagon. The back was filled with clean, fresh hay for the horses to eat. In the center, on fresh hay or quilts, we children and the lunch baskets were packed. We were a very scrubbed, very happy and very excited bunch of youngsters. The time for the jubilee had actually arrived!

We always arrived early, before any of the carnival concessions were open. Papa would find a comfortable place to leave the wagon, unhitch the horses and tie them to the back. Then we would look for our friends as they arrived in town.

By midmorning, a big crowd had gathered, so the parade and races would start on the side streets. Anyone who wished could enter. Prizes were given for the best entries in the parade and for the winners in the races. There were potato races, three-legged races, regular running races for contestants of various ages, and contests for catching the greased pig and climbing the greased pole. There was usually a "slide-for-life," which looked very exciting and dangerous.

By this time, the carnival concessions were open. With the races over, the carnival had a chance to get their share of our spending money.

At noon, the farm families met at their own wagons or buggies. Lunch baskets were quickly emptied of all the goodies it had taken so long to prepare.

Then there was the long, wonderful afternoon. Town folk and other farm folks came in until our little town was overflowing. We children found friends to play with. We watched people test their skills at shooting or throwing balls, and we enjoyed all the noise and excitement. We spent our few nickels sparingly so they would last all afternoon. There were ballgames and horseshoe games in the park for the men who preferred them to the carnival.

The carnival stayed open in the evenings, but Papa always left early, so we children could only imagine this part of the celebration.

We could see the canvas twitch and move as if it were alive.

Each day of the jubilee was the same beautiful, wonderful whirl of excitement to us children—all but the last day. Toward evening on the last day, a balloon ascension took place at the edge of town.

We needed no loudspeakers to know when things were getting exciting out there. Everyone told everyone else, and soon a huge crowd had gathered around the balloon. It looked like a piece of smoky, dirty canvas staked to the ground, but we all knew about the deep hole beneath it, holding a coal fire. This formed hot air to fill the balloon.

As we watched, we could see the canvas twitch and move as if it were alive. Then slowly, very slowly, it would bubble and rise. It seemed to us as if it took hours for the balloon to fill, but each minute was a thrill. Even seeing the man who was to ride in it was exciting. We all stared at him as if he were from another world.

Finally, the balloon was full—standing tall and round, way up above our heads. The crowd was cleared from one side and the man crawled beneath it. Other men pulled all the stakes that held it down. Then oh! the thrill of seeing it float away, the man fastened to it by straps, his legs dangling beneath as he waved to the crowd.

Out across the country he floated, until he looked like a tiny speck under the balloon. Then the man finally disappeared, leaving just a tiny, toy-sized balloon hanging in the sky. He returned to earth by slowly letting the hot air escape from the balloon.

Then it was time for us to start home. Knowing that the excitement was over for a while, we were a very quiet bunch of youngsters in the wagon.

Life on the farm was so lonesome and commonplace for a few days afterward. Letdown feelings and blue depression were everywhere. But that never lasted long. Soon we were gathering junk to make merry-go-rounds, concession stands, and so on. The six of us would soon have our own private jubilee. ❖

—Originally published in May 1966.

Fetching the Cows

By Laina McLaughlin

When I look back to the Good Old Days, I always remember the fun Ina, my older sister, and I managed to derive from the daily task of fetching the cows home from the pasture late in the afternoon.

We were allotted this job as soon as our parents felt we were old enough to handle it. From early May until mid-October, we skipped down the lane, hand in hand, on our way to fetch the cows. We passed through dandelion blossoms, through buttercups and daisies, picking pretty sheepkill and devil's paintbrushes, until the stately goldenrods began to fade. In the sunshine or wind, the fog or the rain, we went each day and loved every minute of it.

Sometimes we would stop to swing the slim white birches or bask on the sunny ledges, dreaming of the future while a soft wind soughed through the tall pines growing nearby. I still remember the warm roughness of the stone against the bottoms of my bare feet. How we raced along those crooked cowpaths that twisted and wound through the alders! Once, I planted a bare foot firmly on a fluffy pink thistle. I screamed as Ina patiently pulled the spines out.

One day stands out in particular, from the summer we were 8 and 10. As usual, we hurried down the lane to the pasture bars. We noticed that the bell cow was missing, so we let down the bars and started the others up the lane to the barn. We listened intently for Mynni's bell, but all we could hear was a neighbor's cowbell to the west of us. We had learned to distinguish the sonorous clunking of Mynni's bell from all others some summers before after

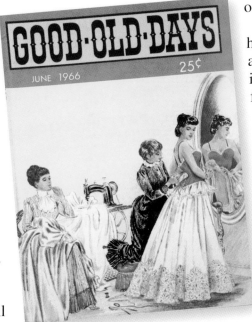

tracking a cowbell to its source over a line fence into a neighbor's pasture.

After combing the pasture over, we decided the lost cow could be in only one place—the gloomy pine woods. We had to crawl some of the way, for the pines grew close and thick and seedlings shot up everywhere. The lower branches were scratchy, and we hitched along on all fours on a thick carpet of pine needles.

After searching for over an hour, we were discouraged and almost ready to crawl back into the sunlight and go home for help. Then we heard a strange, low sound. It didn't sound like a cow, but we headed in that direction. We pushed aside some underbrush, and there—not more than 10 feet away, in a small clearing—lay Mynni, licking a newborn calf.

We sat down and waited until the calf could manage his wobbly legs before starting the arduous chore of going back through the pines with the calf and cow.

Later, as we trudged up the lane, pushing and nudging Mynni's reluctant calf ahead of us, the last rosy rays of the sun slanted across the weathered shingles of the barn. Mother and Father stood at the open linter doorway with milk pails in their hands. They smiled at their wayward girls and spoke soothingly to the distraught Mynni, who made it plain that she didn't appreciate the way we had taken over her pride and joy.

It is well over 40 years ago since Ina and I went fetching the cows home from the pasture, but it seems only yesterday. It is my treasured memory from the Good Old Days. ❖

—Originally published in June 1966.

Two-Bit Artist

By Gracia D. Booth

I never could carry a tune, but when I was about 12 years old, my Sunday school teacher decided that she had discovered a fine alto singer in me. I did not agree, and neither did Dad—he knew that I couldn't sing. But finally, after much persuasion, I reluctantly agreed to perform with three of my schoolmates.

We were scheduled to make our debut on a certain Sunday morning at the local Methodist church. All the other town kids were sure to be in the congregation for this unusual entertainment, regardless of their denominational status.

Dad was dubious but had little to say. Mother was elated at the "believe it or not" prospect of her long-legged, awkward tomboy actually singing in public. As the dreaded Sabbath day drew ever nearer, I grew ever more and more apprehensive—with Dad's full sympathy, although he encouraged me in every possible way. But he knew I'd never make a singer.

We started out fine, sailing through the first verse and chorus of *The Great Judgment Morning* in perfect harmony. About halfway through the second verse, instead of keeping my eyes on my hymnbook or on the floor, as the minister's wife had repeatedly cautioned us all to do, I surreptitiously "peeked" toward the back of the church where sat all the boys and young men.

My sister's mischievous beau caught my eye. Folding his hands devoutly on his stiff white shirt bosom, he rolled his eyes heavenward.

Immediately, I tripped over a flat and completely lost the tune! Instead of keeping still until I could swing back into line unobtrusively, I panicked and searched high and low for that elusive lost tune, throwing the others off-key, too. That is, all but the high soprano. She kept right on through that mournful chorus:

And oh, what a weeping and wailing,
As the lost were told of their fate;
They cried to the rocks and the mountains,
They prayed but their prayer was too late.

I was far too scared to pray, and there was neither mountain nor rock handy to hide behind. Overwhelmed with a badly misplaced sense of humor, I began to snicker behind my hymnbook.

Minnie, my special pal who was seated right behind me, kicked me. "Ouch!" I wailed loudly—and as though my untimely exclamation had been a tuning fork, the others all started in on the third verse, singing in beautiful harmony.

That was the last straw for me! Dropping my hymnbook with a thud and scorning the steps, I leapt over the chancel railing in true tomboy fashion and streaked down that long, long center aisle, cutting for home and Dad. Under sharp wire fences, over ditches and down rutty roads I tore like a young dust devil, in my white-stockinged feet, my shiny, new, high-heeled, patent leather pumps swinging from either hand.

Poor Mother did not scold, as I expected; she just looked terribly disillusioned and sad. Hugging me tightly for a moment against the comfort of her familiar apron, her eyes filled with sympathetic tears. Dad's kindly blue eyes twinkled and his mustache twitched suspiciously as he walked quickly out toward the barn, motioning for me to follow.

Out of sight of the kitchen door and Mother, he furtively slipped a shiny new quarter into my hot, dirty hand—and quarters were mighty scarce then, too!—with the gruff comment that he knew just how I felt; never could sing himself. I gathered that he admired me for trying.

I grew up to marry a Quaker minister. Just before I started that long, long march down that same long, long center aisle toward that same scary platform, the officiating minister, beloved shepherd of my childhood days, patted my arm and softly whispered for only me to hear, "Gracia, a very serious and solemn ceremony is about to begin. I do hope you can manage to stay put. This is once in your life that you don't dare cut and run for home and your dad!" ❖

—Originally published in June 1966.

Some of My Memories

By Ida Derr

It generally used to be that *men* traded horses. But I was a woman who wanted a horse of my own, and I dealt with a horse trader that did not have very high principles. Seems like the poor old horse I bought from him had been pawned off on first one farmer and then another; everyone knew she was balky, and they couldn't do a thing about it—and there were tales of some crude methods used to try to break her.

Anyway, some people felt sorry for me. Others just had a good laugh.

I had two little boys about 3 and 4 years old then, and they loved horses as much as I did. We petted this horse; the little boys fed her sugar and candy. And they couldn't think of eating an apple without giving the most of it to their horse, Molly. I also saved dry bread and any leafy vegetable trimmings for her.

We had a nice, warm barn for her and saw to it that she was properly bedded at night. The little boys started to ride her. She nuzzled them in thanks for their petting. They could and did walk under her and she'd never move.

Finally, I got a little one-horse buggy and harness for her and began to drive her around. I curried and petted her almost as much as the boys did. She followed any of us and seemed always to want to be with us. We even warmed her drinking water if it was too cold. And she never again balked with us.

One day, I drove her to a town 12 miles away. One the way home, she pulled over to the side of the road. We were going through heavy timber and I thought, *Uh-oh, she's going to balk on me now.* I looked around, and there, just a short distance ahead of us, coming out of the timber, was a black bear. The horse never moved, and my boys and I were too scared to. We had never seen a bear in the wild before. We just sat and watched.

The bear nibbled around on roots for a few minutes, then went back into the timber. The little horse then started up and fetched us home.

We had a tall tale to tell about the bear. When the neighbors asked me how big it was, I said, "Well, she was bigger than Molly." How they laughed at me! But to this day, 50 years later, I still say that that bear looked bigger than any elephant I ever saw! That was bear country, and bears did kill cattle and horses sometimes.

My balky little horse never balked with us—except that one time, when she might have saved our lives in that wilderness. I'll never believe that a balky horse can't be cured with the right kind of treatment.

When I moved, I had to sell our little horse. By then, neighbors had seen what a splendid driving mare she turned out to be, and I got more than double what I paid for her. I bought a set of silver in remembrance of her. ❖

—*Originally published in September 1966.*

Boys Almost Unsuitable

By Ed F. Smith

The boy who never wore a suit made from one that his father had once owned certainly missed one of life's most cheerless experiences in the Good Old Days. This example of what might be called home economy was practiced in all average families. It was a "waste not, want not" existence shared by boys and girls. Everybody knew it was a well-kept secret in most households.

There was Willie Brow, for example. His first "made to order" jacket and breeches were fashioned by his mother from Willie's father's wedding suit.

The rather heavy material was a striped combination of dark brown, tan and dark blue. When Father had marched down the aisle in this tailor-made creation of the Gay Nineties, he had been the most conspicuous person in the wedding party. If such a pattern were worn today, it would be described in some quarters as a bit too loud.

However, just before the turn of the century, stripes were all the go.

Father had given this suit little wear after the nuptial vows were exchanged. It hung in an upstairs closet beside Mother's wedding gown. Seeing the two garments each time the closet was cleaned, Mother decided that her spouse's little-worn coat and pants would make her boy a nifty suit.

Of course, she had to get her husband's approval first. After all, he might have become attached to that part of his wardrobe, which had played such an important part in his connubial career. But Pop said it was all right with him, so the die was cast.

The first obstacle Mother encountered was the discovery that moths had attacked the seat of the breeches. In the old days, when holes developed in clothing, the most logical solution was to sew on patches to cover the hole.

In this instance, Willie was much more fortunate than many other boys whose fathers' suits were cut down for them because *his* patches actually matched the material. Mother, being a skilled seamstress, made the repairs

GOOD·OLD·DAYS

35¢

MAY 1967

MOTHER'S DAY

without exposing the stitches. Had there not been sufficient cloth to match the original fabric, a patch or two of a different color or weave might have been used. This would have been regarded by the kid who had to wear the patched pants as a dead give-away. He had to be careful not to stoop, lest the patches showed, which would have been a breach of etiquette in the breeches, so to speak.

In such a predicament, a jacket might have to be made longer, which would sort of put the coat and pants out of balance.

When this story originally appeared, it was illustrated with the cartoon above. The story included this editor's note: "Here is a wonderful old-time story to complement Erwin L. Hess's nostalgic *Good Old Days* cartoon. We believe that you will like these unusual reminiscences about a phase of the everyday life in the beginning of this century."

Another hazard encountered by mothers in making over a large suit to fit a son who also was a trifle on the stout side—taking after Papa—was to discover that the pant legs or the coat sleeves—sometimes both—had to be made shorter to compensate for the lack of sufficient material.

That's why some boys appeared ill at ease. Their bare knees were inadequately covered by the pants or the knee-length black stockings that were held up by round elastic garters. Tight short pants and a coat straining at the buttonholes caused many a boy to develop an inferiority complex, which sometimes lasted until his first ready-made long pants were given to him as a present when he entered high school.

What a grand and glorious feeling it must have been for a lad to wear garments complete-ly free of patches for the first time since he had stepped out of diapers!

Some boys, especially those who enjoyed an old-time game called follow the leader, had hard luck with their clothes. Through some miscalculation, such a boy, while completely clothes conscious when he left home—and despite the warnings of his mother to exercise care while playing—would find himself trying to slide down the trunk of a shagbark hickory tree just because another lad had done it.

Any old-timer who had such an experience as a boy can well recall how the shards of a shag-bark hickory tree would not only turn new pant legs into ribbons, but would also take off much of the underlying skin. *Wow.* What a feeling!

Is it any wonder that overalls were the most popular garb for most of the male population under age 15 in the Good Old Days?

Early overalls had bibs, too, held up by attached suspenders. What an important part those bibs played! They were just right for carrying concealed apples "borrowed" from a neighbor's orchard or cookies from a jar in the home kitchen or a forbidden dime novel to be read while reclining on the hay in the barn loft. Overalls could be patched and patched and nobody seemed to give a darn! It was the stock-ings that needed the darning. Remember? ❖

—Originally published in May 1967.

The Record Sitting Broad Jump

by Don Buchan

Papa was a great athlete. This will come as a surprise to the many old-timers who knew Dick Buchan, but he once made the world's greatest broad jump. Not the running broad jump. Not exactly the standing broad jump, either. Papa operated under a great handicap. He did it from a sitting position. I can give you an eyewitness account, for I was there. You may even agree that I should share the credit, for I helped in an indirect way.

Papa used tobacco in every form. He was seldom without his pipe. It became so much a part of him that he grew absent-minded about it. Sometimes he searched for it when he had it in his mouth.

Mother frowned on the use of tobacco and induced Papa to offer $1,000 and a gold watch to any of their children who abstained from the use of tobacco until the age of 21.

My brother, Skinny, three years older than I, came closest to winning the award. He didn't use tobacco until he was 9.

We were living on East Seventh (now Ninth) Street in Spencer, Iowa, and there was the usual barn where Papa stabled his horses. Between the barn and the house there was the customary small building. I call your attention to it because it played an important part in Papa's great leap.

Skinny concealed the tobacco and some wooden matches in his pocket.

I must have been 6 or thereabouts that day when Skinny filched some tobacco from Papa's humidor in the parlor when we were home alone. He invited me into the small outbuilding to watch him smoke. I accepted with alacrity, as any 6-year-old boy would have done.

Skinny concealed the tobacco and some wooden matches in his trouser pocket, and we marched to the tiny building. Once inside, he clumsily rolled an unwieldy cigarette, using a page from the handy Montgomery Ward catalog for a wrapper.

When he had the monstrous cigarette burning, smoke filled the wee building. At every other draft, the paper burst into flame. When I accepted Skinny's invitation to "try a puff," it made me cough, and tears ran down my cheeks. But according to our boyish code, I would have been branded a sissy if I fled, so I remained as faithful and true as Eugene Field's little toy soldier.

When breathing became difficult because of the cloud of smoke, I sought fresh air by placing my face close to the crescent-shaped opening in the door. There I could peer outside and occasionally suck in a breath of smoke-free air. We heard the sound of an automobile—a rarity in those days—but as Papa didn't own a car, we weren't unduly alarmed until it came panting, puffing and rumbling into the yard. At the wheel of the Ford touring car was Glen Hurd, who was demonstrating the horseless carriage to Papa with an eye toward making a sale.

"There's Papa!" I whispered hoarsely. Skinny turned and, with a snap, tossed the huge cigarette down through one of the oval openings in the wooden seat. Then we made our way to the house.

"I'll pick you up after dinner, Dick," Mr. Hurd said. "And you can make up your mind then." Papa only waved in dismissal; he appeared to be agitated and in a great hurry.

Instead of coming directly to the house, he strode with determination to the little outbuilding. Skinny and I watched through the kitchen window, pop-eyed with fear because tiny strings of smoke still floated lazily around the small building.

But to our amazement and obvious relief, there was no reaction from Papa.

He seemed oblivious to all but his immediate and pressing concern.

How much time elapsed I cannot state, but it seemed only an instant

before Papa crashed out of the doorway as if propelled by some gigantic and invisible power.

That's how Papa broke the record for the sitting broad jump. I think he would have shattered the record for the 100-yard sprint, too, had not his feet been tangled in his fallen trousers.

Skinny ran outside and grabbed the wooden bucket from which the horses drank, and by the time Papa had pulled up his suspenders, Skinny had extinguished the fire in the little building.

When Mother returned that evening, she noticed that Papa walked with the stiffness and

care of a man who had sat on a bumblebee. "What in the world is the matter with you?" she asked.

"I got singed," Papa said. "In the backhouse. The paper caught fire under me."

"I knew it was bound to happen," Mother said sagely. "You go around dumping ashes out of that old pipe without even knowing what you're doing. It's a wonder you haven't burned the house down around our heads long ago."

"But I don't think I was smoking when I went in," Papa protested.

"You smoke so much you don't know whether you're puffing on that old pipe or not," she retorted.

Supper was eaten with a minimum of conversation. Papa had the quizzical expression of one who hears the drone of distant bagpipes. That evening he carefully placed a soft pillow on his favorite chair before sitting back for his first after-supper smoke.

His eyes had a far-away look as if he were lost in contemplation of some occult Hindu philosophy. Now and again he shook his head slowly from side to side with an air of resignation as if he had suddenly been confronted with the fact that there are things beyond the ken of mortal man.

Skinny and I moved about the house as silently as wisps of smoke. We were careful not to disturb Papa's reverie. We seemed to have learned that there are times when a fellow shouldn't tell everything he knows. ❖

—Originally published in April 1968.

The Old Wood Box

By Alice K. Montin

I can remember when every family had a wood box in the kitchen. It was as much standard equipment as the dishwasher or disposal is now. For "renters" (an early-20th-century term for "transients"), poor families or careless, shiftless ones, it was an ordinary carton or wooden packing box of some kind. But the better middle-class families usually had a box with a hinged cover quite frequently made of 4-inch wainscoting and painted an innocuous, uninteresting gray or cream color. It was usually large enough to serve as a seat, and consequently it was crowned with a squashed velvet cushion that had once been plum colored when it was used in the parlor.

The wood box was the extra chair in the old-style kitchen where visiting clergy or neighbors would wait while you finished eating. Neighbors' kids would sit on it with legs dangling, not quite able to touch the floor, so that they would kick it a little until your mother would make some remark about scuffing the paint off with their heels.

Naturally, it was the task of the boys in the family to keep the wood box filled. When you lifted the lid, you found it nearly full—but never completely—with kindling and heavier pieces of wood, all cut just long enough to fit. To bring the box to capacity there were last week's newspapers, often twisted tightly to make them burn like kindling, or folded neatly along one side.

Some people even put a little coal inside their wood box, but to the followers of the pure wood box cult (to which most families we knew seemed to belong) this was heresy. Coal was too dirty to put inside a wood box. Instead, when we could afford it, coal occupied an honored position right next to the stove, filling a brass coal scuttle.

No matter if down underneath a layer of shining Black Diamond or Castle Gate there were old newspapers. No one saw them.

They were just like the stuffing in the bottom of the Easter egg baskets. It was the coal on top that mattered.

And the scuttle in winter must be kept full. In my childhood days, a full coal scuttle in the kitchen was the true status symbol. A painted wood box showed respectability, but a brass coal scuttle full of coal—*that* was affluence. ❖

—Originally published in April 1968.

Remedies I Remember

By Mrs. Pearl Kelley

eading *Good Old Days* has taken me back again to the things my memory holds dear, back to the farm near Johnstown, Pa., where my father and mother lived with their eight children. I would like to share some of the remedies and cures that were used in our home. Herbs and teas were gathered in the fall in case we needed them through the winter. We gathered catnip for babies, pumpkin seed for kidneys, boneset for chills, ginseng for dyspepsia, horehound for coughs and colds, and pennyroyal to promote perspiration. Flaxseed was on hand to remove dirt from our eyes, and, of course, there was sassafras tea to thin our blood in the spring.

At first my father made his own salve, which was used on man and beast. I don't know all the ingredients, but I do know he used beeswax, tallow, carbolic acid and buds from our balm of Gilead tree. Only one of us eight ever got the croup. That was my second oldest brother. We felt so sorry for him as we watched him gulp down a tablespoon of goose grease.

Someone said to make a poultice for her from a swallow's nest.

Then there was my sister who got quinsy. Someone said to make a poultice for her from a swallow's nest. Her beau crawled up into the eaves of an old barn to get the nest. How much he must have loved her to risk his life! They have been married now for over 50 years.

My mother put the nest in a pan and covered it with milk. She let it boil down until it was spreadable. Every now and then she would lift the lid and look in. What an odor! What a stench!

When it was thick enough, she spread it on a cloth and put it around my sister's neck. It smelled up the whole house, but it worked. She never got quinsy after that.

One day I broke out in a rash. My father hitched up the horse and buggy, and we started for the doctor's office. About halfway there, we met the doctor. They talked for a few minutes, and then we all went into a grocery store. They took me behind the counter.

At that time, most dresses buttoned down the back. It was all right to open my dress, but when the doctor unbuttoned my panty waist, that was too much. That was my first experience with humiliation, and I sobbed my heart out.

Then I heard him say, "It's the itch"—as if I didn't know that! (Picture the grocer and his wife, waiting on customers, with the doctor, my father, and me with the itch behind the counter!)

While he was getting my medicine from his satchel, my father buttoned me up, took my hand and led me around to the front of the counter, where he bought me 5 cents' worth of pink lozenges. We then started for home. I took the medicine, and that evening I got a good rubdown with buckwheat flour before I was tucked into bed.

We got the usual treatment for colds. A blanket was put around our shoulders. We bathed our feet in hot mustard water in a wooden bucket. My parents had their own method for administering castor oil. The patient's head was tilted back, and when the nose was held shut, the mouth automatically flew open. When the last of the castor oil gurgled down our throats, we came up for air. Then we were hurried off to bed, where our mother had a warm bed waiting for us, heated with a "smoothing" iron.

At that time very few operations were performed at the hospital. They were taken care of at home, either in bed or on the kitchen table. Ice caps were used for appendicitis. Going to the hospital was something rare.

Dr. Russell, a specialist from Chicago, came to our town once a month to do operating, and so it was that my brother was scheduled for an operation for appendicitis. I shall never forget the anxiety in our home.

The day began early as my father and mother had to drive three miles to the streetcar, and then transfer in town to get to the hospital. My father was never late for anything, so they arrived on time for the operation.

Our grandma stayed with us. I was sent to school, but all I could do that day was sleep and cry. I don't remember having any classes. I think the teacher was pleased to have me sleep.

The day dragged on. It was late when my parents arrived home that evening. They looked so bent from the cares of the day. Over and over they told the story to our friends and neighbors. My father felt he could not trust the doctors, so he donned a cap and gown and went along into the operating room. He then turned my brother over to the doctor and said, "Doc, he's in your hands."

My brother's appendix was put in a little bottle containing alcohol, and they brought it home. My father set it on the sideboard where we could all see it. Every time I went into the room I looked at the little culprit that had caused so much trouble.

After our relatives, neighbors, and friends had all viewed it, my father took it from the bottle and cut it open. Inside was a piece of a toothpick. To be sure, no one ever felt like picking their teeth after that. As I look back over the past 50 years, what a change has been made in the medical profession!

I find it a little amusing that we ever survived. But heaven forbid that I should belittle my good parents, who spent a lifetime teaching us right from wrong, and who sat at our bedside when we were sick, mingling their prayers with faith and hope; or the kind neighbors and friends, who came down the road, up the lane and across the fields with their cures and remedies.

Those were the days, when people practiced the Golden Rule and cast their bread upon the waters. ❖
—*Originally published in June 1968.*

Our Rolltop Desk

By William C. Bierley

At age 3, I loved to hide under our rolltop desk—that grand cubbyhole that was so safe and so warm. Life was great. In 1920, children came down with every ailment in the books: mumps, scarlet fever, chickenpox, measles, and the seven-year itch.

After I had been home sick from school, a boy came to see me and tell me the news. He said, "Charles—well, you know, he has the lice. A lot of kids got them."

"Oh Mom!" I moaned. "And he sits with me!" Mom laughed for many years over the way I said it. She didn't have much to laugh about. Moms had their hands full raising a family in those days. Their family came first, and their thoughts only wandered now and then to the mortgage.

Sis caught the measles, and the doctor was coming. I started for my hiding place, as usual, but I was itching and feeling sick. The doc came in with his heavy pill case and started upstairs, only to turn and come over to the desk. He reached under and pulled me out, saying, "You get upstairs. You've got them too." I went up crying.

As the years passed, a lot of family living took place around that dear old desk. Pop sat there every night making out blacksmith bills during the Depression—bills people couldn't, or wouldn't, pay. Pop and Mom grew old. Finally their last sickness came, and they are sleeping now in the town's cemetery—a sleep of the just.

I often think of when I grew too big for my hiding place. There was a sadness knowing I no longer could hide from the world.

The day came, all too soon—sale day—when they carried out my rolltop desk. I brushed away a tear or two as a part of my life passed out that door. I would never again know that special joy of childhood, of crawling under that old rolltop desk. ❖

—Originally published in November 1968.

Old-Fashioned Christmas Tree

By Dorothy Jordan

It stood in the corner, stately and tall;
Loved by the children, admired by all;
With fragrance of woodland filling the air,
It seemed that the forest was actually there.
For month after month, preparations were made,
And now, Christmas morning,
the artwork displayed.
The family had fashioned, from paper and glue,
Long chains in colors of every bright hue;
Strings of popped corn and cranberries red,
And fat little men of sweet gingerbread;
Cornucopias and bags filled
with hard sugar candy,
And icicles shaped from any foil handy.
Entwined through the branches, tinsel so bright,
It sparkled in glimmer of soft candlelight;
On top of the tree shone the beautiful star
Like the one which had led wise men from afar;
Balls of fine glass (from abroad, we were told),
Red, green, blue and silver, and sparkling gold.
Much you have missed, you will have to agree,
If you never have seen an old-fashioned tree.

—Originally published in December 1968.

My First Airplane Flight

By Jeannette Rutledge

Perhaps this letter written by my cousin, Mrs. Georgia Hawkins of Indianapolis, to her sister about 1917–1918 will be of interest to some of your readers.

Dear Virginia: —

Am sending you under separate cover a couple of pictures taken of me upon return from my airship ride. It was this way—I had watched that airship buzz over my head so often that I just simply *had* to go up in it. So I hiked myself down to the inlet and just climbed in and went. And such a wonderful ride it was, too. First they give you cotton to stuff in your ears, then a red woolen hood that covers all but your face,

Above: Mrs. Georgia Hawkins seated in her plane, not a bit timid if you please, even though the plane looks like something put together in a basement. Inset right: The flying boat, Alantic City, N.J., 1915.

and a brown woolen coat; then you climb in and they button an oilcloth over your skirt to protect it from the spray, for the first part of the ride is over the water up the bay.

The machine holds three. One can sit in the back, but just the aviator, who you see in both pictures, and myself went up. The ride out over the water is grand; it must be something like going fast in a motorboat. Finally he turns around and starts back. Then you go faster and faster until the boat lifts from the water and begins to ascend. You go up and up. We were 1,600 feet above the water, but when you get up, it seems like you are creeping along, although he said we were going 45 miles an hour. You look over and can see what you are passing and can then realize that you are really going faster than it seems.

The only inconvenience is the strong wind in your eyes. You have to squint all you can. You can't talk, for the other party couldn't hear you, but you can hear the whir of the machine coming behind you, and the different winds sort of rock and sway the boat.

No, you are not frightened. You want to whip it up and go faster and faster. You look over the side and such a grand view, on one side, way out over the ocean—on the other, Atlantic City and the meadows and mainland beyond. How small and insignificant the island looks. It seems just a step across it.

The trip is from the inlet, a little beyond the Million Dollar Pier. On the way up, we sailed over the ends of the piers and on the way back, farther out in the ocean. There is something so fascinating, exhilarating about it all, you just want to keep on going.

The glide from the air down to the water again is the best thrill of all. You know the sensation you get on those deep dips of the roller coasters when they drop down a steep incline? A thrill starts in your toes and comes up and up and seems to go out the top of your head.

Well, it's just like that, only longer, and then you are back skimming along on the water

again, and the spray splashing out on each side. All too soon you are back. It's all over, and, yes—you are disappointed that you have to come back to earth. When you get back, there is a man there to snap your picture. I did not see him at all when he took the one climbing out and the other either until I heard someone say, "Look this way, please!" and it was over. My face was all squinted up and my eyes were so windblown I look like I was jagged.

Well, it was all just wonderful and must be experienced to be appreciated. I would love to go again, but I won't because it's too expensive. It was extravagant of me to go once, but you can do anything once.

The rest of the day I went around in a trance. I think I really was pouting because I had to come down to earth; the rolling chairs, the moving pictures, the people—all were so tame and commonplace. The aviator is a young Frenchman. He is quite tall, but small featured. He says every time he goes, it has the same fascination for him.

I said, "Oh, how I love that coasting or gliding down to water."

He said, "It's the up part that gets me."

Well, it *all* gets me.

Love, G.

In a later letter to me, my cousin Georgia wrote that it was her first airplane ride—her first and last, and added:

"Glad I got that far in the air anyway."

I had my own first airplane ride in Iowa in a little plane flying over Twin Lakes on Labor Day in 1919. As I recall, my 10-minute flight cost $20. I could have had five more minutes of stunt flying for $10 more, but I had no desire to have the plane turn somersaults in the air.

Before going up, I had to sign a document promising not to attempt to collect any damages or to allow my executor to collect any if anything went wrong during the flight. (Nothing did.) ❖

—Originally published in January 1969.

My Mother's Bible

By Jim Clark

On one of our shelves, surrounded by books of all kinds on various subjects, stands an old book in a cover of plain paper. It's not very attractive to the eye and seemingly out of place among the other books that stand by its side.

Its covers are worn; its leaves are marred by long use; yet, old and worn as it is, to me it is the most beautiful and valuable book that I have. No other awakens such memories or so appeals to all that is best in me. It is, or was, my mother's Bible, which was the companion of her best and holiest hours, source of her greatest joy and consolation. She derived from it the principles of a truly Christian life and character. It was constantly by her side, and as she grew older and her eyes grew dim with age, it became more precious to her.

The time came when this good pilgrim passed on beyond the stars and beyond the morning and entered into the rest of the eternal Sabbath. And now, no legacy is more precious to me than that old Bible.

Years have passed, but it stands there on the shelf, a witness of a beautiful life that is finished. In moments of weakness and fear, it says, "Be strong, my son, and quit yourself manfully." Sometimes, when my heart is heavy with the cares of this world that seems so hard, selfish and unfeeling, and the strings of my soul have become un-tuned, I seem to hear that book saying the well-remembered words of a voice long silent: "Let not your heart be troubled."

There is no need to take the book from the shelf or open it; our memory of it and our associating with it supply the rest. We now and then read of modern scholars and their opinions and of the many versions they propound, but they are quickly laid aside and the plain old Bible that was my mother's is taken from the shelf. In a few days now we will celebrate Mother's Day again. Won't you please take down that old Bible, not only that day, but every day, and be in quiet, peaceful prayer for all mothers? ❖

—Originally published in May 1969.

What My Mother Taught Me

By Mrs. Mabel Fischer

As Mother's Day comes again, I think of my kind and good mother who taught me so many useful things— how to work and be happy and be thankful for things that were ours. She showed us the beauty of sunsets and wildflowers. With kindness, we to care for animals on our farm. What happy times we had!

There were 10 of us, and each had to work. We were taught to never pass the wood pile empty-handed without carrying some to the wood box. We had to pick berries, hunt greens, help wool the sheep, and stir the apple butter out in the yard—which was a hot job, since it would stick if not stirred a lot. We also made our own soap.

I remember the baths on Saturday night in the old washtub behind the kitchen stove, and the work we had on Saturday to get our clothes ready for church the next day. I remember the cold and mud, walking to school over that long country road. I remember when I mistakenly took the bucket of lard to school instead of my lunch bucket, and how the children all shared their lunch with me since it was too far to walk home.

We each had our jobs on Saturday. I had to polish the brass bands on our water bucket with salt and vinegar, clean the coal-oil lamps and churn the butter—but how good it was on the bread Mother baked through the week! All our food was cooked on that big old cookstove, which we all had to carry wood for. Before we left for school, we each had to rub some clothes on the washboard so Mother didn't have all that rubbing to do.

I could tell you so many other things that my wonderful Mother taught me. I hope I have been as good a mother as she was. In my wonderful memories, I say to her, "Yes, Mom, your work was well done." ❖

—Originally published in May 1969.

Something New At the Wedding

By Gracia D. Booth

When I was 8 years old, my bosom pal, Emmy, was to be flower girl at the church wedding of her big sister, Irma. Practically everyone in the community had been invited. Emmy had a dream of a dress—sheer and ruffly, and it came clear down to her new white sandals. She had long, white, silk mitts, too, and a cute little pink straw bonnet to match her dress.

I had a special new dress, too, but not long and fussy like Emmy's. Mother would play the organ, and my preacher daddy would perform the ceremony. Daddy insisted that I sit by my mother, behind the organ, completely hidden from Emmy's sight. I would have to peek around the organ to see what was going on.

The ushers had shown the last guests to their seats, and the church was packed when Daddy, Ray (the groom), and the best man came out of Daddy's study and solemnly took their places in front of the altar.

Unnoticed by anyone but me (and I sure didn't let on), my little dog, Fido, had managed to sneak in at the half-open side door and creep under my chair. Then Mother swung from the soft strains of *To a Wild Rose* into the slow, solemn chords of *Here Comes the Bride*. That was just too, too much for poor Fido, whose canine ears were attuned only to *Jesus Loves Me*, *Brighten the Corner* and such hymns, for he always tagged along with us to Sunday school.

Darting out of hiding before I could stop him, he made straight for Daddy and, squatting down in the aisle right in front of him, threw back his wooly head and howled mournfully.

Ray's face got as red as fire and the best man was trying not to grin.

Ray's face got as red as fire, and the best man was trying awfully hard not to grin. Overwhelmed by embarrassment, Father simply glared in my direction. I sat frozen to that chair until, in desperation, Mother lifted one toe off the organ pedal and kicked my shin.

It was up to me to do something—quick! I dashed out from the shelter of the organ and grabbed Fido, who began to bark furiously at this further indignity. Snickers and giggles could be heard from all over the church. I was afraid to go out the side door—it was too close to Mother, and her eyes were spitting fire.

The only other way out was along that rose-petal path, and without a moment's hesitation, I headed that way at a breakneck gallop, almost upsetting Emmy who was halfway down the aisle. In full sympathy with Fido and me, she tossed her half-empty basket toward Daddy and, hoisting high her long, fluffy skirts, scurried at my heels. Scattering rose petals, we tore through the procession and out the open door.

We hid under the bridal wreath hedge at the back of the church until we heard everyone leave for the reception at Emmy's house. Nobody looked for us, and we were too scared to go, so we missed it all—all but the scoldings we got that night when we ventured home.

Emmy and I were not quite sure that Irma and Ray were really married after all that ruckus—and without Emmy doing her part—until the twins arrived. Then we decided they must be. And when the babies were named for us-Emma and Ella—we knew at long last that we were fully forgiven. ❖

—Originally published in June 1969.

My First Car

By Edith LaFrancis

My first auto was a Model T Ford, which I bought with my own money. I was a 4-H Club leader and spent my summers dashing all around my hometown of Agawam, Mass., inspecting gardens, poultry projects and egg records. I also taught canning and organized the fall exhibits, so my little Model T roadster was just the thing. The rumble seat opened up in the back and often overflowed with 4-H members on the way to meetings.

The picture was taken in 1928. The car was a 1926 model, as I could not afford a new one. It was one of the last of the Model T's; the following year, Henry Ford put the Model A on the market.

Incidentally, the house in the background of the picture is the farmhouse that my grandfather bought in 1869. Hidden among the grapevines up over the hood of the car is the window of the room where I was born. My father was also born in this house. The grapevine was a tangle of several Concord and Niagara vines, and by 1930 it had reached to the attic window. The smell of the tiny blossoms in spring and grapes in autumn filled the house with a rich, sweet perfume.

On the day I bought the car, a friend of mine, Walter LaFrancis (who later became my husband), went with me to the dealer's lot and helped make the big decision.

The author poses in her first car, a Model T Ford that she bought with her own money.

We were assured the roadster was in excellent condition. That night, we set out blithely for a real trail spin, taking some of the back roads down into Connecticut. I was driving, with Walter cautioning me a bit on the curves. He could always see better than I in the dark. I always seemed to discover dips and curves in the most unexpected places.

There was nary a streetlight, of course; only the magneto lights of the car, dimming and brightening, and a myriad of fireflies to make tiny pricks in the velvet black of a summer night. Merrily we hummed along, the air current of our speed touching us only gently because of the fashionable wind deflector sported by this snappy model.

But gradually a growing noise developed in the left front wheel. Walter diagnosed it immediately, and commanded, "Stop. Pull over. Dry bearing!"

I did as I was told. There we were, miles from nowhere, with a car we had supposed to be in top condition—and it couldn't be driven home without grease in the wheel.

"Well," said Walter, "let's see what there is for tools."

We opened the rumble seat and climbed in. The tools were kept in there on the floor. With a lighted match to aid us, we looked over a jumble of spare parts— tire pump, tire-patching kit, jack, a couple of wrenches, a tire iron and a round can. Walter opened the can hopefully. "Ha! Grease," he exclaimed. "Somewhat dirty and old, but we can use it."

Taking out the wrench and jack, he proceeded to take off the offending wheel, more by sense of touch than by the light of the matches I lit. He packed the grease in and replaced the wheel, and we were on our way home, by the shortest route and with him at the wheel, complaining only mildly about salesmen in used-car lots.

That was the beginning of many exploits and journeys for the sturdy little car. On one occasion, it took us all the way to Cape Cod, a distance of 200 miles. Let your memory travel back if you can and feel the jolting and vibrations a Model T seemed to transmit from a bumpy road to the human anatomy. After a trip

of that distance, even the young could discover they had muscles and joints! However, the little car was a whiz on the Cape's sandy byways.

We didn't attempt to drive it on the beach. One of our friends there had a 1914 Model T in which he ventured out onto the sand at low tide to the spots where he had his clam beds. (He planted baby clams, and when they grew, he dug them up again and shipped them in barrels by train to New York City.)

I remember many other rides, like going up over the Notch in Amherst, where I had to keep my left foot on the pedal to hold the car in low gear for more than a mile. I remember coming down hills so steep that I used low gear as a brake. There were sudden storms when it was necessary to snap on the side curtains. There were cold winter days and nights with snow driving in around the curtains—and no heater, as I remember.

The windshield wiper wasn't perfect, and there were times when the only way to drive was to let down the window and lean out. The rain, sleet or fog collected on my face and hat while my hands and feet still managed to control the wheel, gas lever, clutch and brake.

Repairs were needed frequently on any car in those days. Tires didn't last as long as they do now, and it was a common sight to see a driver sitting beside the road, putting a patch on an inner tube. I don't remember doing that, but I could change a tire if I needed to.

As to cleaning the carbon and grinding the valves, my friendly mechanic took over that job, and on more than one occasion, completed the process in a Saturday afternoon and evening. By the time he finished, I would be tired of watching and handing him tools. But he seemed to enjoy working on cars and had had plenty of practice repairing his own, a Model T touring car.

As happens to all cars, their usefulness must come to an end. When Walter and I were married and had a new car, we loaned the roadster to cousins who took it out to the lake where they had a camp, and where a winding dirt road roamed in and out among dense woods. The cousins had learned the way so well that either by day or pitch-black night, they could navigate merrily in and out and over tree roots and rocks. Passengers in the rumble seat gripped tight to keep from getting bumped against the metal edges where the upholstery was either flimsy or did not exist at all. But the very hazards and insecurity of such travel often brought shrieks of excitement and gales of laughter.

Bit by bit, spare parts fell off the old Ford, and finally it had to be given over to the junk heap. It is long gone now, but the memories remain of its adventures in which it played such an important part years ago, when my life was in its springtime. ❖

—*Originally published in August 1969.*

A True Friend

By Marjory O'Neal

As a very young child on a farm south of Otis, Colo., about 1931, I sat by the window and watched my sister and three brothers leave for school. They all rode together on one horse. One brother rode in the saddle, my sister sat behind the saddle, and the other two boys bounced along behind her. I wondered where *I* would ride when I started to school with them. When I began first grade, I found out.

My first year in our country school, named after my grandfather, found me climbing into the saddle with my brother, Allen. Two of us fit pretty snugly in that saddle, but I felt very safe and secure. My sister rode behind me and carried a large lunch box containing food for all five of us. My youngest brother, Bill, sat behind her, and my oldest brother, Ronald, rode on the tail.

Our horse, Prince, was very patient with all of us. When Ronald slid off once in a while, Prince would stand quietly while he ran and jumped back up on his back.

One day as the five of us were riding slowly to school, crossing the neighbor's field, Allen, the brother guiding the horse, decided it was time to gallop awhile. When he kicked Prince in the sides, Prince jumped and all five of us fell off. My sister fell on top of the lunch pail.

As we gathered ourselves up off the ground, the horse stood waiting for us to continue our trip to school. We found it a little painful sitting in our desks that day because of the bruises. Prince stood in the barn all during our classes, and then, blizzard or sunshine, took us safely home at the end of the day.

Sometimes he got loose. Then he stood inside the schoolyard fence, waiting; when he saw us go out to close the gate and catch him, he immediately made a run to escape. We had to run fast in order to beat him to the gate. Sometimes we didn't make it. Then he would stay a short distance ahead of us all the way home— just far enough so we couldn't catch him.

Prince carried us to school for 13 years. He was truly a trusted and faithful friend. ❖

—*Originally published in August 1969.*

Helpful Aunt Dollie

By Clara Comstock

The year was 1913; I was 10; and the place was a farming area north of Van Buren, Ark. Our maiden aunt, Great-Aunt Dollie, was a real doll. She was the family's "helper-outer," always on hand on baking day.

The trouble was, she wasn't a very good cook. Her piecrust was terrible—and in these parts, every woman was proud of her feathery, light, white cakes and flaky, light piecrust. Mama said Aunt Dollie had "too heavy a hand" on her piecrust, and after I watched her pound and wrestle with it, I guess she did.

Saturday in every home was baking day, and Aunt Dollie made the rounds of the family to help. On this particular baking day, when it came time for her to help us, she donned her gray-striped apron and rolled her sleeves up. Then she shooed all the little kids out of the kitchen, but she let me sit on a high stool and watch.

She got out the big wooden bread tray, sifted it full of flour, made a little "well" in the middle, got a handful of hog lard out of a stone jar, worked it with her fingers, added a second handful, worked it, then sprinkled a bit of salt and sugar, and added a beaten egg, then cold water a little at a time to make a stiff dough.

She soon turned it out onto a bread board. She kneaded it over and over, singing "Glory, glory, hallelujah!" as she turned it with the heels of her hands. She finally turned it over, smiled and gave it a little pat! Then she stepped to the back door to dust off her hands, slipped on the step, and sprained her ankle.

We helped her to a cot on the porch. While older sister fixed a poultice, Mama slipped into the kitchen and made a new batch of piecrust.

Mama used to say of me, "That Clara has to have her finger in the baking," and so she gave me the leftover dough to make "nibbles." Now, nibbles were leftover piecrust with butter, cinnamon and brown sugar sprinkled on. Cut into strips, it was such a treat for us children!

This time, I had such a gob of dough, and how good it felt as I squeezed it, and how grown-up I felt as I rolled it out, while little brothers Carl and Vernon watched.

I spread soft butter on half of it, sprinkled brown sugar and cinnamon on it, then folded the other half over, rolled it again, and repeated the same thing. I folded and rolled it out four times, then buttered, sugared and cinnamoned it, spread it on a cookie sheet, cut it in bite-size pieces and baked it. Everyone thought those nibbles were so good.

After that, I got to make nibbles every baking day. I've improved it since that long-ago time, but the basic dough is just about the same. I taught two daughters and two granddaughters how to make nibbles. Now I'm starting on the fourth generation, as Kelly Ann, age 5, tiptoes to the table and begs, "Let me pat it, Mamaw"! ❖

—Originally published in September 1969.

Old Cloe and the Bull

By Nelson E. Thomas

I have often told about this incident at family get-togethers, but somehow I never found time to put it down on paper. But it is such an unusual story, with a final outcome so unlikely, that I feel it really should be told. I was born and reared on a farm in southwestern Iowa, and these events took place when I was 9 or 10 years old. We had a driving horse named Cloe, who was of good racing stock and a really good trotter. Her disposition was not what one would call bad, but she did dislike our big red bull, and she chased him at every opportunity.

Lauren, my brother, who was just older than I was, seemed to consider this set-to great sport, but our dad took an entirely different view. He laid down a rule that Cloe was not to be turned loose in the yard if the bull was there. In such a case, Cloe had to be led to water and then put back in the stable or into another yard.

"Let's turn out old Cloe," he said, "and have some fun."

One fine frosty Saturday morning, Dad had to go into town with the team and wagon for supplies, and left Lauren and me to finish the chores. We were working away, cleaning out the horse barn, when suddenly Lauren got a gleam in his eye. "Let's turn out old Cloe," he said, "and have some fun."

I have to admit that I probably was not of much help to my brother in this moment of temptation. Anyway, we opened the barn door that led into the large, square barnyard where the bull was, and Cloe's halter rope was untied. As she stepped through the door, she spied the bull, calmly eating at the feed rack not more than 20 feet away. Cloe flattened her ears and made ready for the attack.

The bull happened to look up just then and saw what was about to happen. He whirled, put his tail in the air, and took off—not quite in time, however, for Cloe managed to give his rump a good nip.

By the time Lauren and I had climbed the yard gate so as to have a ringside seat, the show was in full swing. Cloe took that bull around the yard full tilt, and believe me, he was going all out. Even so, Cloe somehow managed to catch up about every fourth jump and give him another good nip.

On one side of the yard, we had a long cattle shed with a large open door in the middle. One end was enclosed for a hog shed, with a ramp leading from the cattle shed up into it. On the yard side of the hog shed, there was a long high window. As the bull came tearing around the yard, letting out a healthy bellow each time Cloe caught up with him, he saw this cattle shed door. Evidently thinking "any port in a storm," he pounded through the door, up the ramp, and without one faltering step, apparently decided the window was his only way out.

Alas, the window was too small and too high, and although the bull came through, he brought most of the side of the shed with him, in splinters.

Lauren took one good, saucer-eyed look at the side of the shed and decided we might just as well make a clean breast of the whole thing with Dad when he arrived home. However, after looking the damage over carefully, we decided that we might be able to patch it up so that it would not look quite as bad as it did, scattered all over the yard. We got a hammer and some nails and went to work.

Piece by piece, splinter by splinter, we fitted the side of the shed back together. When we finally finished, we smeared some mud over the cracks and on the heads of the shiny new nails. It was a good job, if I do say so, and unless one was looking for it, the repair hardly would be noticed.

I can assure you that we worked like beavers, both at the patching job and at trying to finish the work that had been laid out for us for that Saturday. We failed to finish all our tasks, but I guess Dad was in a good humor when he got back from town that day, for he did not say too much about it.

The next day, being Sunday, we were allowed to "sleep in" (till about 6 a.m.). Dad, however, was always up bright and early, regardless of rain or shine or the day of the week. He no doubt liked to get out by himself once in a while to size things up, without interference from his small fry.

On this particular morning, he decided to turn the horses out to water before he started milking. Somehow he forgot all about Cloe, and he turned her out, too.

Well sir, as near as Lauren and I could put it all together,

old Cloe again stepped out of the barn door, spied the big red bull eating at the feed rack and made her dive for him. And once again, the bull whirled and ran with Cloe right behind him, getting in a nip often enough to keep him right up there at full speed. Down around the yard they went, into the same cattle shed, up the ramp, and out through the side of the hog shed, again taking out most of the side.

By this time, Lauren and I had arrived at the barn to help milk, and Dad came in, telling us all about it. You could tell that Dad hated to admit that he had forgotten about the rule concerning Cloe—and, of course, Lauren and I just listened in wide-eyed silence.

But the payoff came when Dad remarked, "I just don't understand all those shiny new nails in that old lumber." ❖

—Originally published in December 1969.

Christmas At Grandmother's

By Bertha Leonard Davis

Christmas was a wonderful day at Grandmother's. Uncles, aunts and cousins started arriving the day before, some by train, some by sled or sleigh. Our family arrived by train. Grandfather or one of the uncles who still lived at home met us with the sled. Grandmother had heated sacks of oats in her big oven to keep us warm on the ride to the farm. There were shawls and blankets and, on occasion, the old fur robe. It was indeed a privilege to have the old fur robe to wrap up in.

Once we were settled all comfy and cozy, Grandfather or the uncle picked up the lines and clucked to the horses. They needed no extra urging; they had been stamping, snorting and champing at the bit while we were snuggling down in our blankets. Now, away we went.

Usually we were the last to arrive, since we lived farthest away. When we arrived at the big old farmhouse, we were warmly greeted by Grandmother and all the rest. She bustled around, helping us remove our wraps while inquiring solicitously if we were cold or tired or hungry. Then, while maintaining a continuous line of chatter, she seated us at the kitchen table.

Then she served us a bountiful supper—a large bowl of fried potatoes, home-cured ham, coleslaw and homemade bread spread with freshly churned butter. Then, to finish the meal, fried cakes and molasses cookies were topped off with coffee for Father and Mother, and hot milk with a lump of butter floating in it for us children.

After we had eaten, we separated into groups—the women in the kitchen, the men in the sitting room, we children in the two rooms upstairs reserved for us. Upstairs, there was still more grouping: the young folks (they weren't classed as teenagers then), and the youngsters from ages 6 to 12. The babies had been left downstairs with the women, and some of the little boys had stayed with the men.

When finally we had caught up on all the news since last we had been together, our thoughts and conversation turned to the big tree that stood in the parlor behind closed doors. Much speculation took place.

Later, the house quieted down. Some of us were too excited to sleep, but nevertheless we lay quietly, waiting for morning, when at last we would get a chance to gaze upon that marvelous tree.

No matter how early we planned to get up, Grandfather had been up long before to start the fire in the kitchen range, and stoke up the fires in the stoves in the dining room, the sitting room and the parlor, and Grandmother was busy at the kitchen stove, preparing breakfast.

As soon as Grandfather and the boys came in from doing the chores—for the animals must be cared for, even on Christmas Day—breakfast was served and eaten rather hurriedly because even the adults were feeling the excitement of the children, though none would admit it.

At last the parlor doors were opened. Everyone crowded in to gaze upon the tree, and they all agreed it was the biggest ever. (As I think back, however, I seem to recall that that was an annual observation.) From his own woodlot, Grandfather had sought an evergreen tree so tall that it touched the ceiling. The branches were perfectly formed, the needles thick. Strands of popcorn and cranberries garlanded those branches; oranges, apples and popcorn balls hung from the branches. Colored candles also were placed at intervals on the tree, but never lighted. Grandmother would not permit it—too much danger of fire.

When all expressions of admiration were exhausted, Grandfather distributed the gifts, commenting humorously as each gift was passed. Most of them were homemade, even the toys, but oh, the thrill each experienced as his or her name was called.

Delicious odors began permeating the whole house. Grandmother, the daughters and daughters-in-law had slipped out to the kitchen by twos or threes to prepare the dinner while all the commotion was going on in the parlor. It took some time to present the gifts, since they numbered about 40 people, counting the babies.

Finally, all the adults and babies were seated at the huge table in the dining room. The rest of us stood around quietly while grace was said, thanking God for all our blessings. We young folks and children again adjourned to our special rooms until the adults had finished.

Delicious odors began permeating the whole house.

Later, we were called to a freshly set table. I don't know how she managed it, but Grandmother always had plenty of food. There were platters of goose, duck and chicken, bowls of snowy white turnips, mashed potatoes and rich brown gravy, Hubbard squash served in its own green shell, baked beans, bowls of dried corn that had been soaking most of the day before and all night to restore it to its golden plumpness. After it was cooked, it was covered with thick, rich cream.

There were dishes of cucumber and apple pickles, glasses of blackberry and dewberry jams, tomato and groundcherry preserves, plum and apple jellies. For dessert, we chose mincemeat (homemade), pumpkin or apple pie—or all three, if we could manage to eat that much. While we ate, the women washed the dishes from the first table and visited. When we had finished eating, the older girls washed the dishes and straightened the dining room and kitchen, chattering and giggling all the while.

In the afternoon, babies were put down for their naps. The little children played with their new toys. The young folks once again went to the upstairs room to talk of the things most interesting to young folks. Some of the boys and men took a walk around the farm while the women sat and visited.

There was plenty of food left and everyone lunched when they felt like it. There was coffee on the back of the stove and lots of milk in the buttery for the children, so no evening meal was prepared.

After evening chores were done, we all gathered in the sitting room, some around the organ where the aunts took turns playing, and we all joined in singing, mostly hymns.

At last the day was over. Those who weren't staying the night left for their homes, while the rest of us retired to rest for our long trip home the next day. As we drifted off to sleep, we all acknowledged that once again, Grandfather and Grandmother had given us another wonderful Christmas Day. ❖

—Originally published in December 1969.

The '70s:
The Memories Continue

Chapter Two

*G*ood Old Days has for many years been associated with its wonderful covers depicting so many of the scenes of Americana. From the parlor where the radio was the center of entertainment to the meadow where a quick spring shower wasn't enough to dampen the joy of an afternoon picnic, the participants in our covers always look for the brighter, if sometimes bittersweet, side of life.

Entering the 1970s, the magazine was still looking for a definitive cover style. Sometimes, in the 1960s, cartoons were employed on the cover. Nostalgic photographs were tried for some issues, but *Good Old Days* needed an artistic signature to hang its hat on.

That signature was found in the paintbrush of an aspiring young artist by the name of John Slobodnik.

Ed Kutlowski, founding publisher and editor of *Good Old Days*, first commissioned John to paint covers for the magazine in 1972.

With a style reminiscent of Norman Rockwell, John gained national exposure for his graceful, nostalgic work. In all, he completed dozens of paintings for the magazine.

I remember first seeing John's work in the early 1970s when I was a reader, not an editor, of *Good Old Days*. I was immediately drawn to John's work.

Little did I know that, in less than 20 years I would be collaborating with John on magazines and books. As *Good Old Days* moved into the 1970s, it was John Slobodnik's artistry that best defined the magazine's heart and soul.

Today John paints from his studio in Illinois.

—*Ken Tate*

Above: *Rain, Rain Go Away* by John Slobodnik, House of White Birches nostalgia archives
Facing page: *Good Old Days* magazine cover, February 1973, House of White Birches nostalgia archives

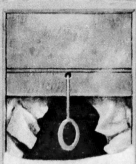

50¢

November 1973

46490

GOOD·OLD·DAYS

Featuring: LETTERS * STORIES

·PHOTOS * POEMS * CARTOONS * SONGS * ILLUSTRATIONS *of the Happy Days Gone By*

John Slobodnik

The Flimflammed Sibling Strikes Back

By James J. Yellen

When I was a kid, like any other kid whose attention span peaked at somewhere around eight and one-half milliseconds, I went through phases during which I would devote every waking hour to one sole pursuit. For example, there was one summer somewhere between infancy and puberty during which I did nothing but play Monopoly.

For three months, Duke, Chuck and I did absolutely nothing else. From 8 in the morning, when we met on Chuck's front porch, until late evening, when we had to strain our eyes to see by the meager light from the street lamp, we would roll the dice and move our lead markers.

Underage financiers, we bought and sold and bought again. Play money changed hands at a pace that would make J.P. Morgan's head spin. Only impassioned pleas from our mothers could make us pause to take nourishment. With our bellies filled, we would rush back to resume our shylocking.

What's it going to be today? I would ask myself. A walking corpse?

There was also my chemist phase, wherein I spent all my time mixing up the chemicals in my A.C. Gilbert chemistry set; and my bowling phase, and my pool phase. But no time in my life is more memorable than the several months during which I ate, drank and slept *Inner Sanctum*.

Inner Sanctum was a radio program that dealt with unbelievably horrible and unspeakable things such as ghosts, ghouls and murderers. I loved it! Every Monday by 8 p.m., I had worked myself into such a frenzy that my hand actually trembled as I reached to turn the switch on our table model Emerson. Glassy-eyed, I would sit staring into the faint yellowish glow of the dial, waiting for the sound of the squeaking door that introduced the show each week.

"Squeeeak!"

When that door creaked, my pulse quickened and tiny beads of perspiration formed on my brow. Even today, years later, I still retain the reflexes for which I was conditioned as a boy. The mere sound of a door hinge chirping starts my adrenaline flowing and my temples pounding.

What's it going to be today? I would ask myself. *A walking corpse? Or maybe an ax murderer. Or will it be some indescribably hideous monster?* Whatever it was, I ate it up.

Facing page: *Good Old Days* magazine cover, November 1973. House of White Birches nostalgia archives

And then there was Raymond, "your host." Raymond was a guy with a sense of humor that bordered on the obscene. Who else could make such digging remarks about graves? And his delivery! Raymond delivered puns like Henny Youngman delivered one-liners. He put them up for grabs. If you liked one, it was yours, but if you didn't, all you had to do was wait, because he would have a dozen more.

Why such a show appealed to me, I'll never know. Raymond's holy retreat had absolutely nothing in common with Athenia, N.J. We had no haunted houses in Athenia, no zombies, no cackling witches. The world in which I lived was nothing like Raymond's, but I was hooked on *Inner Sanctum* nonetheless.

My brother was a fan of *Lights Out*, another popular radio show of the time that dealt with tales of horror. Pablum for mewling babes! Saccharine! *Inner Sanctum* was the real stuff!

Then there came one Monday night that changed my listening habits. The week before, during his preview of coming attractions, Raymond had promised an unusually scary story. I couldn't wait. All that day at School No. 13, while Miss Moran chattered on and on about long division and the Battle of Trenton, my mind conjured up images of voodoo rites and gypsy fortune-tellers.

The day dragged on. Several times I seriously wondered if 8 o'clock would ever come. It seemed so far off. At supper, I pushed the franks and beans around my plate, unable to eat, my stomach tied in knots from anticipation.

In our house, getting to listen to *Inner Sanctum* required incredible scheming and long-range planning. I was a kid brother. Being a kid brother isn't easy, and around our house it meant that I had second choice in what we listened to on the radio. Therefore, Monday nights required ingenuity.

Immediately after supper, I rushed into our bedroom. Plopping myself onto my half of our bed, under my full-color photo of the entire Brooklyn Dodgers baseball team, which I had torn from the Sunday *New York Daily News,* I switched on the radio.

Instantly sensing that I was getting one up on him, my big brother, Charlie, dashed into the room. "What are ya listening to?" he asked with the naturally superior attitude that goes with being the senior sibling.

"Whatever you want to," I babbled meekly. I played my part perfectly; Dustin Hoffman could take lessons from me.

"Good," he said, spinning the dial across the stations to tune in *Tom Mix*. Now I had him hooked; all I had to do was play him right, and I would land him.

After *Tom Mix*, I humbly acquiesced as Charlie switched to the sports report, then to the *Beulah Show*, then to *The Lone Ranger*.

But then, about midway through the Wheaties commercial, at about a quarter to 8, I cleared my throat and asked in a quivering voice, "How about we listen to *Inner Sanctum* next?" I was reeling him in.

"Naw, you listened to that last week. Today, I'm listening to *Straight Arrow*." He was playing into my hands nicely. I almost had him in the boat.

"Yeah, but you been listening to what you want all night. Ma, Charlie's hoggin' the radio! He won't let me listen to anything I want!"

That did it. My mother entered the fracas and after hearing the facts, she took my side. She had to. I was right because I had set him up. It worked every time. Charlie never wised up.

"*Squeeeak!* Good evening, friends, this is your host, Raymond, to welcome you through the creaking door to the Inner Sanctum! I'd like you to meet some new guests that we've just— dug up!"

Wow! He was in rare form tonight.

"And don't forget, many are cold, but few are—frozen."

Raymond was incorrigible.

On this night, my tactic had, for some reason, particularly incensed Charlie. After Mom's declaration that we would listen to *Inner Sanctum* instead of *Straight Arrow*, Charlie pulled his baseball cap down over his eyes and sat stone-faced and cross-legged on the bed. I could tell that he really meant business because this was a position that he usually reserved for visiting relatives and the milk of magnesia bottle.

There was no doubt about it. He was mad. Perhaps he was beginning to realize that he was being taken. But I paid no attention, for my eyes and ears were nailed to the speaker.

"Tonight's story is about murder … murder and a clock. So if you've got a little time to kill, let's do it, huh? A timely story, wouldn't you say?"

The story was of a creeping clock—a cursed antique timepiece that killed whoever got in its way. Each of its victims died hideously screaming as the ticking of the homicidal clock grew louder and louder until the *tick-tick-tick* of the timepiece overtook the cries of the unfortunate victim.

Raymond had outdone himself this time. The show had been so realistic that it caused me to cast a wary eye at our old Big Ben wind-up sitting there on the nightstand. I wiped my sweaty palms on my dungarees. Fear made my palms sweat. Imagine that—a creeping, killing clock.

Charlie remained in his comatose state until bedtime was announced. He still remained silent as he prepared for sleep. I paid little attention to him because thoughts of Raymond's ramblings were still in my mind.

After settling down under the covers with all the house couched in darkness, I was just starting to drift off when suddenly I heard Charlie whisper. "Sssssssshhhhh … did you hear that?"

"Hear what?"

"That ticking."

"What ticking?"

"That ticking. Don't you hear it?"

"That's the clock."

"That's the Creeping Clock!"

"Aw, come on," I said. "That's just our clock."

"No, it's not. It's the Creeping Clock, and it's coming in here to get you! Tick, tick, tick!"

I tried pulling the pillow over my head. That worked for a short time, but it wasn't long before I could hear the ticking again.

"Here comes the Creeping Clock through the door now," Charlie persisted. "The ticking's getting louder! Tick … tick … tick …"

"Ma! Charlie's scarin' me!"

That brought our mother into the room. When she asked what was going on, Charlie, of course, denied all my accusations. Mom went back to bed, leaving strict instructions to "Keep quiet and go to sleep." But after she had gone, Charlie started again: "Tick, tick, tick!"

It was about this time that I became aware of a tingling feeling inside. *Oh no!* I should have gone before getting into bed! Now I'd have to make my way across the house to the bathroom, and I was scared stiff!

> *I was just starting to drift off when suddenly I heard Charlie whisper. "Sssssshhhh … did you hear that?"*

Reluctantly, I dragged myself out of bed and started on my way through the blackness. My knees trembled. My palms were sweaty.

"Where are you going?"

"I-I have to go to the bathroom."

"Watch out for the Creeping Clock!"

Oh, why did he have to say *that*? I made my way as fast as I dared, anxious to care for my needs and get back to the safety of my bed. As quickly as I could, I made the first leg of my journey without incident.

It was half over and all I had to do now was make the return trip. Cautiously I felt my way down the hallway toward my room. It seemed even blacker there now with my eyes unaccustomed to the dark after the brightness of the bathroom. Safely I made it to the bedroom door. Only a few more steps and I would be back in bed.

Suddenly, as I groped my way into the bedroom, something, some strange thing, reached out and grabbed me! What was it? I let out a scream! "Yeooow! It's got me! The Creepin' Clock's got me!"

The following Monday night I found that I just didn't feel like listening to Raymond anymore. Somehow that old feeling was gone, and I discreetly switched my loyalties to the *Great Gildersleeve*. Life in Gildersleeve's house wasn't as exciting as life in Raymond's Inner Sanctum, but it was a whole lot safer. ❖

—Originally published in November 1973.

Almost Tango Champ

By John T. Raymond

*I*t all started when I was 12 years old and our family had moved from a big, old home in the country to a townhouse, which we rented from a dentist who was getting a divorce. The house was located in a neighborhood of Irish and German Roman Catholics. Down the street about three doors was a pretty girl named Dodie Schultz.

We were about the same age, and—perhaps because I was a new boy—Dodie made a big play for me. Soon we started going to dancing classes together.

That was all right with me, as Dodie was a popular number and I was just swinging into the romantic phase. However, there was a catch to our otherwise happy relationship: Dodie's family.

I never saw her father. I think he had a job in the paper mill that kept him away from home during the daylight, and he played poker every night. It was Dodie's mother who was the fly in the ointment. She was a born matchmaker, and she had maneuvered Dodie's older sister, Maxine, into and out of four marriages. I didn't like the speculative look in her eyes when Dodie and I were together.

> *The Waltz was next. Dodie and I cut a mean rug on this number.*

As for the dancing class—we learned a lot of steps there. You know, the old two-step, waltz and, yes, the tango. The tango was my nemesis. Being about 5 feet 5 inches in height, I wasn't very adept at a dance that called for all those long glides and bends; nor was I the Latin type like Rudolph Valentino, who was the top tango boy at the time.

Anyway, there was a public street party to celebrate the opening of the town's first new hotel since the Civil War. One feature of the program was a dance contest.

Dodie's mother and sister persuaded me to go with them, "just to watch," they said. Right then, I learned never to trust any girl's mother, because the next thing I knew, Dodie and I had been entered in the dance contest.

The first number was a two-step. About half the dancers were eliminated right off, evidently because they couldn't count.

The waltz was next. Dodie and I cut a mean rug on this number. We slipped in some fancy twists and turns that I'll bet the Viennese never even dreamed of, and we ended in a tie with a taxi driver named Pete Smith and his girlfriend.

At this point I began to get scared because I suspected the judges would probably call for a tango, and, sure enough, they did. To complicate matters, I had caught sight of my parents at the edge of the crowd, and my mother looked like it does before rain. She didn't approve of Dodie, and even less of Dodie's mother and "Marryin' Maxine."

Then there was the other couple. Pete Smith was half-Indian, tall, dark and handsome and a smooth dancer. His girlfriend was right up there with him. Furthermore, some of my friends in the audience were giving me the horselaugh and prancing around, imitating the tango.

I tried to argue Dodie into forfeiting, but it was no go. She had a grip on me that her mother must have taught her. There was no escape.

About that time, the orchestra swung into a Latin rhythm and off we went. You may remember the drill—how you do a series of long, slithery glides, bend over your partner like a dentist looking for cavities, and then repeat the same business in the opposite direction.

After a few turns up and down the space cleared for dancing, to the accompaniment of shouts of "Atta boy!" from my friends, I wanted out so badly.

Besides, there really wasn't any competition. Pete and his girl tangoed as though it were their main form of exercise.

They were just going into a beautiful, swooping bend when it happened. Pete's foot caught on a piece of loose pavement, and he fell right on top of the girl.

That did it for her. She scrambled to her feet and before Pete could get her back into position to continue, she let him have a solid right to the jaw that sent him sprawling again.

The music stopped, and I noticed one of the judges bearing down on Dodie and me in a purposeful manner. I guessed what he had in mind, and I didn't want any part of it. All that razzing from my friends was bad enough, but the thought of seeing our picture in the paper as winners of the dance contest—with, no doubt, Dodie's mother and Marryin' Maxine in the background—was just too much.

So I told Dodie I was going to borrow a handkerchief from my dad, and I dashed off, neatly dodging her mother and that man-crazy sister, who wasn't about to let any man get away, no matter how short or young he was.

I found the family car and discovered my mother had come there before me, having guessed my intention. We drove off, and we did not stop until we reached Grand Rapids, 90 miles away.

We stayed with friends for a week, then returned to find that my father had had to foreclose on our former home, and we were already moved back in.

I quit dancing class for a while and gave Dodie's neighborhood a wide berth.

Naturally, I wanted to forget about that dance contest, but my friends remembered. One of them brought me a copy of the local paper, published the day after.

It had a picture of Pete Smith, sitting on the pavement where his girl had floored him. One of the judges was handing him a trophy, and the caption read: "Local man wins dance contest sitting down." ❖

—*Originally published in April 1974.*

Uncle Walt's Last Fight

By Walter Jackson

The article entitled "New Boy in Town" prompts me to tell of my own experience in boxing, way back in 1921, and that's 53 years ago. I was a member of a dance orchestra, four musicians and a banjo player. I was the banjo player.

By a strange coincidence, three of the four musicians were expert boxers. Jerry, the saxophone player, was an amateur boxing instructor; Graham, the violinist, had sparred with Benny Leonard; and Reggie, who played drums and xylophone (the manager pronounced it "sloppophone"), was a promising light heavyweight with plenty of amateur experience. But the only one who owned a set of boxing gloves was me—who knew nothing at all of boxing—so I took them along to the summer resort near the American border where we had a full season's engagement.

None of the pianists we had took any interest in the manly art, perhaps from fear of hand injuries, but I was not going to lose any chance to get free lessons from experts.

We had lots of time on our hands during the afternoons, so we used to box in the dance hall. It had a roof, but no sides. The two combatants would stand, not sit, in two imaginary corners. One would holler "Bong!" as we had no gong to start the round. If either of the combatants wanted to quit, he would holler "Bong!" and that was the end of the round.

We took turns boxing each other. Either I was a slow learner or they were fast teachers. I hollered "Bong!" so often that it became second nature; but as the season advanced, I improved a bit and made a name for myself. That name was "Battling Linoleum" because I spent so much time on the floor.

At last the season was drawing to a close, Labor Day being the finish. On the Saturday before Labor Day, a newcomer booked into our boardinghouse. He was a nice, likeable chap named Bob. He had heard that we boxed a bit and asked me if I would care to take on a round with him. I agreed. He was much shorter than I was, and I felt confident I could hold him off, owing to my longer reach.

That name I made for myself was "Battling Linoleum" because I spent so much time on the floor.

It was a cool morning, and we both wore turtleneck sweaters. None of the orchestra boys was around, for which I was sorry. I wanted them to see how much I had improved under their expert guidance.

I said "Bong!" and he went "Bang!" Round one was over. There wasn't any second round. It was two minutes before I could breathe.

Later in the morning, the sun came out and it got warmer. Bob discarded his sweater, and for the first time, I was able to study his arms and shoulders. They resembled, more than anything else, the hindquarters of an Army mule!

After the last dance on Labor Day night, I said goodbye to Bob and I gave him my boxing gloves. I have never worn any since. I found out later that his job was polishing huge slabs of marble at a nearby quarry—by hand! "Bong!"

The moral of this story is: Don't quarrel with a quarry man. Also, if a man has an old-age pension, he should give up boxing. There's no future in it! ❖

—Originally published in June 1974.

The Sweet Scent of Summer

By Georgia H. Smart

The shrill chirp of katydids always gets to me. Add to this the soft glow of a street lamp filtering through the leaves of a big maple tree, the sound of children playing down the block, and the creak of our old porch swing as I relax in the warmth of a summer evening. These combined sounds have the power to transport me back in time over four decades, and I am a child again.

I feel the silkiness of sun-warmed dust as I sift it between my bare toes, the heat of a hot afternoon sun flushing my cheeks and

heating my body. I walk slowly, savoring the smell of the unpaved streets as I near my own home after a day of play with little friends.

And, in the evening, supper over and the dishes done, with the pure pleasure and stamina of the very young, I run and play some more. Then, breathing hard, I sit for a few minutes on the front stoop with the family, my head resting on Mama's knee. We love this time of evening, the quiet, the beginning coolness of the night. We watch the fireflies with their flashing glow and the June bugs batting against the screen door, seeking the inside light.

Then, on the next corner, I hear the sounds of big brothers and friends gathering under the streetlight for games—red light, hide and go seek, kick the can—and I beg to go, too.

I am allowed only the privilege of standing on the fringe of their activity and observing, since I am too young to play, they say.

Too soon, too soon, I hear Mama's call. Time to come in. Reluctantly I head for home, a little sullen because the boys can stay longer.

The soft dust is cooler on my bare feet now. Passing a house, I hear a piano, the sound pretty and bright and happy. I tarry a few minutes and listen with pleasure. I move on past another neighbor's flower garden and stop again—this time to sniff the sweetly scented night air from their flower garden.

Young as I am, I wish these joys would never end. When I walk into our kitchen, tired at last, I dread the chore ahead. I think, *It's so much fun to go barefoot, but I wish—I wish!—Mama wouldn't make me wash my dirty feet tonight!* ❖

—Originally published in June 1974.

Our Fan

By Helen J. Bean

We had one electric fan. To have had two would have been an extravagance. Anyway, about 1917, with our kind of electricity, both of them buzzing away would have blown the fuse!

I knew summer had come when Mother brought the fan from the attic, dusted it, oiled it and placed it in a certain corner of the parlor. From that location, everyone received some of the stiff breeze if we had it turned on "high."

We had an oscillating fan, but some of our friends had the kind that only flew in one direction. Their company either had to bunch up to be cooled or swelter politely outside the fan's range. On the straight blowers, Mother usually was in the front row because she "felt the heat." It seemed to me that "feeling the heat" got you the coolest positions. I always brought up the rear on that kind of deal. I dripped profusely on those hot days, but I really didn't know how to "feel the heat."

In her pocketbook, Mother carried a folding fan as her secondary source of relief. At church, we always sat to the rear near an open window to catch any puff of air that chanced to slip in. Mother was not one to depend solely upon the whimsical forces of nature. She always appeared with her church fan. I enjoyed trying out the various cardboard "coolers" found in the racks on the back of the pews. They came in a variety of sizes and shapes. The ones advertising funeral parlors were the most numerous.

Mother had a fan decorated with sparkles for parties. I always thought it was very pretty, and I have kept it with other souvenirs from those years. There were other fans—one for going to town, one for afternoon calling, and several for other occasions. When Father returned from his business trips in the summer, he often brought her a lovely one.

I could tell how hot it was by Father, who firmly believed that under ordinary circumstances, a man continued to wear his suit coat upon returning home from the office. When he took off his coat and he wasn't even going to bed, I knew it must be getting hot.

He was a "suspender man," so when he slid the left one off his shoulder, loosened his tie and unbuttoned his stiffly starched wing collar, it was *hot*! He knew that heat was a matter of thought control, although he never objected to being cooled slightly by our fan.

At night we used the sleeping porch, but sometimes not a breath of air was stirring. I don't know why it never occurred to us to carry the fan upstairs. It seemed to be an immoveable fixture in the parlor during the summer.

Instead we went to bed with a palm leaf and fanned ourselves to sleep. When that failed, we took our pillows downstairs to our electric fan. I turned it on; that was my job. Each one selected a supposedly cool place and stretched out on the floor for the night.

Father, hoping for a natural, gentle breeze, took his spot near the open front door. In the early morning hours, he usually groaned about how hard the floor had become. With his pillow, he would take off for upstairs and a comfortable bed, while Mother and I would choose the cool over the comfort. I thought it was great fun, sleeping on the floor to "beat the heat."

I still have our fan. Every time I have taken it for a tune-up, the repairman has said, "I think we can get you through another summer."

I cannot remember life without our fan. The only change I notice is that each year, it seems to be a little heavier. Somehow I think that I have missed something through the years, for I never truly learned to "feel the heat." ❖

—Originally published in June 1975.

Facing page: *Good Old Days* magazine cover, June 1974, House of White Birches nostalgia archives

Clang Went the Trolley

By Norman Cheney

When I was a boy many years ago, we lived in a large, eight-room house in a small New England town. We were a large family by today's standards. Six boys and three girls, our ages ran as steps, from 6 to 25. My oldest brother was married and living with his wife at home. Father was a mechanic, repairing shoe machinery. Mother was the hub of the family wheel. She was a little blue-eyed lady, weighing a scant 100 pounds, with energy to spare to care for her family.

One this particular day, she was busy in the kitchen preparing to bake a week's supply of bread. She was turning the handle on the mixer, and her dough was almost ready to be handled, punched and set to rise.

We were whining for something to do, restless, as our summer vacation was drawing to a close. We stood around watching, hoping perhaps that molasses cookies would be on the agenda.

Mother's patience was finally exhausted. She said in a strained tone, "I have an idea that might appeal to you. Why not take the trolley ride around French Hill?"

That evoked a sudden interest on our part. "The idea is good, Mother," I replied, "but we do not have any money."

She hastily answered, "The fare is only 10 cents round-trip. I'm sure there is a quarter in my purse, which you can have."

Poor Mother. It was well worth a quarter to get us out of the house for a couple of hours.

The trolley ride she had suggested was a local Toonerville trolley, a streetcar for local trips only. Its route covered seven miles. Its fare was 10 cents for the round trip. It was a perfect Senior Citizen Special, but senior citizens were unheard of in 1910.

On rainy days, Mother often gave us a dime each for a ride on that trolley for two excellent reasons: It was something for us to do, and it offered a chance to clear the house of noisy children. We would walk the quarter mile to the square and board the car.

The motorman would pull the pole down. This pole had a pulley on the end that rolled against a live wire, furnishing power to the motor. This procedure had to be followed each time the car was to move in the opposite direction.

We took seats in the rear and watched people get on. But I was more interested when someone wanted to get off. I noticed they pulled a rope that ran along the ceiling of the car. One pull would ring a bell up front. The motorman would stop the car. Two rings and he would start up again.

With this knowledge stored in my brain, I decided to have a little fun. I waited until we were well on our way. Then I stood up on the seat and rang the bell once.

The car stopped; the motorman alighted to assist the passenger off. Alas, he waited in vain; no one appeared. He got back on, stuck his head in the doorway, and demanded to know who had rung the bell.

No one answered. I had discovered a new amusement. After that day, I rode the trolley as often as I could produce a dime. If I could scratch up a quarter, I would take brother Bill with me.

This trick worked fine until fickle fate took a hand. I learned a most valuable lesson: Never underestimate a motorman.

One bright sunny day, we boarded the trolley. I failed to notice the new mirror hanging over the motorman's head. This gave him a clear view of the entire interior of the car.

I sat down, blissfully ignorant, waiting impatiently for the car to start. When we had traveled a mile or so, I stood up on the seat for a repeat performance.

I pulled the rope once. The car came to a grinding stop. The door flew open and the motorman, instead of alighting, came into the car. Down the aisle he came and stopped beside me.

Glaring, he took me by the arm and escorted me the length of the car, to the door, where he ejected me with a violent push. He warned me never to set foot in his car again. I never did.

That evening, as Bill and I lay in bed, Mother came in to tuck us in and kiss us goodnight. She said, "Have you been good boys today?"

Bill answered "Yes" quickly, but I hesitated. I did not want to lie to my mother, so I told her what I had been doing on the trolley rides.

When I had finished, she looked at me and said, "Are you happy with what you have been doing?"

I said truthfully, "No, Mother. I think I have been mean."

She said, "Are you sorry?"

I answered, "Yes, I am."

She said quietly, "Then the next time you see that motorman, tell him you are sorry."

One of the blessings of having an old-fashioned mother was that she took the time to teach us right from wrong, and I am truly grateful for that. ❖

—Originally published in November 1975.

My Doll Emily

By June Woods

Hospitals haven't always been the austere, antiseptic places they are today. There was a time, especially in small towns, when a big, remodeled house served the needs of the ill. The staff, if not as professional as today's, generally was friendly and had time to make visitors feel welcome. Even children could come in then instead of being shut out.

But perhaps it's better the way things are run now, for the awful thing I did as a 5-year-old never could happen today.

It all began with Emily.

Emily was my doll, a gift from Uncle Henry, given to help me through a siege of measles. My spots were itching their worst when Uncle Henry handed me the flannel-wrapped bundle.

"Here," he said. "She's had the measles, so you don't have to worry about giving them to her. Take good care of her. She needs lots of love."

It was an easy promise to make. In the doll fashion of those days, Emily's china face was exquisitely detailed with blue eyes and pink-tinged lips and cheeks. My life from that moment changed. Like a mother with a new baby, I continued to see friends and to do the things I had

done before, but not until Emily had been taken care of first. Jump rope had to wait until after her bath or until she was napping in her buggy where I could glance to see that she was all right.

Mama and I spent even more time together. She sewed clothes for Emily while we talked about what babies needed to eat and how to make upset stomachs feel better. The three of us, Mama, Emily, and I, took long walks together.

I liked it best of all when we walked the six blocks to the hospital. The three-story building once had housed apartments and was full of silent corridors, doorways and long stairways. When Mama took me there, we always went up the stairs to the top floor where the new babies were kept. We'd look at them for a few minutes; then Mama would leave me there for a time while she visited someone she knew.

Babies fascinated me. I never wondered how they got there. To me they were just available, like sacks of sugar in the market; when you wanted one, you came here to get it. I never tired of looking at their wrinkled faces peeping through the soft flannel wrappings. I liked to see them stretch and make faces. Sometimes one would wake and cry. Then Mrs. Smedley, the nurse, would come. She was friendly and talkative.

"Hello," she'd say as she checked diapers or laid a baby across her shoulder to pat it. "It sounds as if this little fellow is hungry. I'd better take him to see his mama." And off she would go, leaving me to watch the others.

Sometimes Mrs. Smedley would ask me how Emily was and stop to look at her. Wrapped in her blanket, Emily was almost indistinguishable from the real babies. When she left, I'd show the babies to Emily and talk to her about them.

I'd had Emily just about a year when the tragedy happened. One moment I was sitting on the steps, Emily cradled in my lap, and the next, she was lying on the ground, her delicate face shattered into a thousand pieces. I never understood just how it happened, but I was inconsolable.

Mama was sympathetic, but her efforts to comfort me were futile. Condolences and gifts from friends and neighbors were met with unresponsive politeness. When Uncle Henry brought me a new doll, more elaborate by far than Emily, I would have nothing to do with it. Nothing, *nothing* could replace Emily.

For days I moped around the house and yard, rejecting offers of games and walks to town. Mama was worried, but I couldn't help her. I was too heartbroken to pretend even a little joy. Then one day, as I sat on the step, absentmindedly rocking the empty buggy back and forth, the answer struck me.

I looked around to make sure Mama wasn't watching. I knew she wouldn't like what I was going to do, but she was nowhere in sight. I lifted the latch on the front gate carefully so it wouldn't rattle, pushed the empty doll buggy through, and then slipped out myself.

Once out of the yard, I didn't hesitate. I turned the corner and started to walk the six blocks to the hospital. I only hoped no one would stop me, for little girls don't often get too far from home without someone asking questions. But that day I met few people, and those I did just smiled at the sight of a little girl taking her doll for a stroll.

The day was warm, and when I reached the rambling building, only the screen door was closed. I opened it easily and climbed the familiar stairs. Not until I stood in front of the babies did I meet anyone. It was Mrs. Smedley. I was afraid she would ask about Mama or Emily, but as it happened, she was very busy right then and only said "Hello" before disappearing again behind one of the closed doors.

Then I did it. My heart raced and my head throbbed as I picked up one of the pink bundles. Cradling the baby carefully against me, I went down the same stairs I'd just climbed. I hoped anyone who saw me would think I was carrying Emily, and I prayed that the baby wouldn't cry.

As luck would have it, I met no one. Soon the infant was in the buggy, its eyes open, but perfectly quiet, as if enjoying the adventure.

I started for home jubilantly, but as I neared the house, my doubts began to grow. I knew Mama wasn't going to like what I'd done. I wondered how I could keep her from finding out, at least for a while, but it was too late. Mama was at the corner, looking for me.

"You should tell me when you leave. I was worried about …" Then she saw the baby and I heard her gasp. Without a word, she picked up the baby, grabbed me by the hand, and we started back to the hospital. I remember how strange it seemed that Mama didn't even take off her apron.

Well, it's easy to guess what happened after that. When we reached the hospital, everybody was all excited, but things calmed down soon enough when they saw the baby was safe. But nobody could believe that a little girl had managed to take her without anyone knowing.

After a while, Mama and I went home. She didn't scold me much. She even bought me another doll, but I just set it on the shelf with the others. I never played with any of them. ❖

—Originally published in July 1976.

The Day the Animals Changed Color

By Rick Gates

Running full gallop, the cow lifted its green tail toward the sky, jumped the narrow creek and disappeared into the woods on the opposite side. Grandpa, his old gum boots flapping like mudguards on a semi, was running too fast to stop at the creek. He was also running too slow to jump the cress-lined stream—and the weight of 64 years didn't help. He hit the water like a skimming stone … except he didn't skim.

I had been following Grandpa at a safe distance of 50 feet, and by the time that I arrived at the stream, Grandpa had settled waist-high in the water. He now sat with outstretched legs and appeared to be contemplating the air bubbles escaping from his boots.

"You all right, Grandpa?"

His vivid red-almost-purple face turned slowly toward me. Grandpa didn't answer me, and for a full, two-hour minute, his blue eyes glared into mine. Suddenly a grin broke through the deep wrinkles, and his outstretched hand reached to me. I scrambled down the low bank to help him up; perhaps the way he was grinning indicated that I wouldn't get a whipping.

"Come on, boy. Let's go. That cow won't wait for us to catch up."

As I grabbed Grandpa's hand, his grip tightened, and with a force that belied his age, he swept me into the water beside him—stomach first. Sputtering and confused—maybe Grandpa was going to drown me!—I pushed myself up to a sitting position and looked at him. He pulled himself erect. Then, with water sloshing out of his boots with every step, he scrambled up the creek bank. Turning, he glared down at me. I hadn't moved. I hadn't even breathed.

"Come on, boy. Let's go. That cow won't wait for us to catch up."

With the speed, agility and fear of a 10-year-old, I sprinted up the bank after him. As I ran after Grandpa, I thought about the circumstances that had put me in such a mess. The day had started out fine, with Grandma shaking me awake.

"Rick, time to roll out. Hurry now. Breakfast is on the table." The only word that I heard was "breakfast," but that was enough. I dressed, ran down the back stairs and out through the side door. I made a fast trip to the outhouse. I stopped at the old pump, dashed a few drops of water over my face, then opened the back door and skidded into the kitchen.

"Hurry up, boy; we're waiting," said Grandpa as he speared a big brown biscuit. I sat down and looked around the table—a platter of eggs, some of them brown on both sides, and others with a big yellow eye; a large platter with thick cuts of ham; light brown ham gravy; toast, almost black, from the top of the old wood stove; two pies and a chocolate cake; steaming cups of coffee and a large pitcher of milk; jams and jellies; home-baked bread, and a large brown crock filled with freshly churned butter. For a 10-year-old boy, it was Thanksgiving at every meal.

After breakfast, Uncle Charlie and I headed for the barn. Grandpa was going to a farm sale and wanted us to shell some corn and turn out the stock while he was away. Charlie was only six years older than I, but Grandpa had taught him almost everything there was to know about a farm. About the only thing he hadn't taught Charlie was that a city kid on a farm can get into more trouble than a butterfly in a flock of birds.

Charlie put an ear of corn in the sheller, and I started to crank. We had worked for about an hour and had two or three bushels of corn shelled when I remembered the large metal drum.

"Charlie, what's in that drum that man brought yesterday?"

"Paint. Dad wants to clean up the chicken house next week. Then we're going to paint it."

"What color?" I asked.

"I don't know what color," replied Charlie as he started to crank the sheller again.

"Why don't we go see?"

"Well, I guess it won't hurt anything if we just look at the color," Charlie said.

Corn forgotten—at least *I* had forgotten it— we dashed out of the barn and around the corner to the utility shed. In a few moments we had the lid of the drum pried off, and both of us stared down at the thick brown fluid.

"Sure is an ugly color for a chicken house," I said.

"Stupid, that's oil. We'll stir it up and see what color it is." We found a couple of sticks and started to stir.

Stirring paint in a 50-gallon drum wasn't easy, and five minutes had passed before we saw the first light streaks of green appear.

"It's green, Charlie!"

"I can see it's green. OK, we've seen the color. Put the lid back on, and I'll go back to the barn and start on the corn again." Charlie threw his stick out the door and followed its path.

I continued to stir, fascinated by the light green color. It was then that I saw the old hen and her chicks. Perhaps if that hen had timed her appearance a little later, the following events wouldn't have occurred.

The small, golden chicks were a challenge to my imagination, especially with that large paintbrush so handy on the shelf in front of me. One by one, I cornered the chicks, and with dripping brush, I changed them from gold to green.

The old hen had stood her ground and waited patiently while her brood returned to her, wet and green. The color of the baby birds had perhaps stupefied the old hen, because I had little trouble in catching her next. At least the entire family was all one color now.

I heard Grandma call Charlie into the house to help her rearrange some furniture, and that was the moment that I started to get into trouble.

I thought about the three cows and Old Doll still up there in the barn and the idea hit me. I grabbed a 5-gallon bucket and dipped it half-full of paint. Then, with paintbrush in one hand and the heavy green liquid in the other, I staggered to the barn.

The cows were still chewing on the hay that Grandpa had put in their mangers, and they didn't seem to mind as I brushed first one way and then the other. I made four trips to the large drum for refills before I had completed the job. The drab old Jersey cows were now the same color as the chickens—a nice bright green, from the tips of their tails to the black of their noses.

I was still carried away, but somewhere in my mind a voice said, *Rick, you better turn the cows out before Charlie returns.* Grandpa had told us to turn the stock out. I opened the back door, and one by one, I released the cows and watched them amble outside. I was about to close the door behind them when they let me know how they felt about their new color. With loud bawls and tails in the air, they fishtailed down the pasture and disappeared over the hill. I could hear them bawling as I closed the door.

Maybe I can get Old Doll painted before Charlie gets back, I thought. In no time I had the old workhorse the same glorious color as the chickens and the cows. I led her through the stable door and turned her loose. She trotted a few paces, turned, looked at me, then down on her side she went.

For a few seconds she was quiet, and then she started to roll, first on her back and then on her side. When she finally struggled to her feet, she was covered with straw, grass, cornhusks and whatever was loose on the ground. She shook herself like a dog with fleas, and then, like a green ray of light, she ran to the pasture.

"What in tarnation have you been up to?" Charlie's voice startled me. I wheeled to face him. "Do you know what Dad's going to do to you when he sees those dead chickens?"

"What dead chickens?" I asked, innocence written all over my face—I hoped.

"Those dead green chickens. You know what I'm talking about. Look at you! Paint all over. Boy! Is Dad going to roast your behind!"

Charlie hadn't mentioned the cows and the old workhorse. *What if they died, too?* The thought really frightened me, and I was beginning to regret my actions. Maybe I should tell Charlie about the other animals.

"Charlie … I … uh … I painted … ."

"I *know* you painted those chickens." Charlie cut me off before I could push the words out of my mouth. "Come on. We'll go tell Mom what you did." Charlie gave me a push in the direction of the house.

> *"What in tarnation have you been up to?" Charlie's voice startled me. I wheeled to face him.*

We had covered half the distance when the loud roar of a plane engine caused us to pause and look in the direction of the noise. The little yellow plane was low over the south pasture and headed directly for the woods.

"He's going to crash, Charlie!" I yelled. Charlie didn't answer.

"Come on, Charlie! He's going to crash!"

"No he won't. See?"

Charlie was right. With engine straining, the tiny plane lifted its nose and started a climbing turn. Then, just when it appeared that the plane would clear the woods, the very tip of a tall pine tree caught the down wing, and the tiny craft faltered. Recovering its momentum, it swooped up and over the trees.

"That's just like Tailspin Tommy does it in the movies. Did you see him hit that tree, Charlie?"

"Course I did. Wonder what he was doing down so low?"

"Don't know," I replied. "Maybe …"

The sound of sliding tires in the barnyard interrupted me in midsentence.

"That's old Jim Henry, our next-door neighbor," said Charlie. "Wonder what he wants?"

"Where's your dad?" Henry had directed his question to Charlie, but now he was staring at me. "What's that all over you, boy?"

With the excitement of the plane and the appearance of this old, mean-looking farmer, I had forgotten about the green animals and the fact that I was about 95 percent the same color.

Charlie saved me from answering. "Dad went to a sale over to the Williams place. Said he'd be back around 9. About that now." Charlie squinted up at the sun.

"Well, all the imps of Satan have broken out at my place!" exclaimed the old man. "They're about the same color as this boy here. They came charging out of your woods—through the fences, and past the barn where we were putting up hay. Those horses took one look at those green things and bolted. John was on top of the hay wagon, and he was thrown off. Think he may have a broken leg. Our hay is scattered all over the barn lot, and I doubt that I'll ever get the harness untangled from the horses!"

Charlie bit his lip and continued to examine the large golden dandelion at his feet. I wished that I was back home in town.

"That's not all," continued the bib-overalled figure. "Our Omar man was just pulling into the drive when those whatevers came through, and he tried to drive up that old beech tree. There's bread, rolls, cakes and what's left of a truck scattered all over my front yard!"

I closed my eyes and wished that I could disappear. I opened my eyelids and peeked out, only to find that I was still in the same place.

"The reason that I came over here is that I noticed a crumpled horn on one of those green cows, and I thought of your dad's Jersey." Henry looked right at me. "From what I see, I'd guess that I came to the right place. Right, boy?"

I answered with one affirmative nod.

"You tell your dad to come over as soon as he gets back, Charlie. Better tell him I'll expect some damage money, too." The grizzled farmer yanked the door of his truck open, climbed behind the wheel, started the engine, and then slammed out to the road.

Charlie didn't say a word until the sound of the truck had died away. "You painted the cows, too?" His voice was a monotone of disbelief.

"I painted Old Doll, too." At least the truth was now out.

"I just don't believe it," said Charlie. "I swear, I just don't believe it." The words were hardly out of Charlie's mouth when I saw Grandpa's truck coming down the road.

"Here comes Grandpa, Charlie. I'm going to get a drink of water. I'm thirsty." I wanted to be far away when Charlie told his dad.

I watched from the pump house as Charlie explained what had happened. Grandpa glanced up at the house, and then he and Charlie jumped into the truck and headed in the direction of the Henry place. I could tell Grandpa was mad because he was going almost 35 miles per hour.

I watched until the truck was out of sight. Then I ran inside and sobbed out the story to Grandma. "Now, now. I'm sure it's not as bad as all that," she said.

"Oh, Grandma! I'm so sorry. The chickens all died, and the cows and Old Doll will probably die, too. Mr. Henry is going to make Grandpa pay for his hay, and the bread man will probably want a new truck. Grandpa is going to whip me for sure when he gets back, and …" I burst into tears again.

"Come on now, Ricky. You sit down at the table, and I'll get you a piece of cake and a glass of milk. Stop crying now."

I had finished the cake and milk, and Grandma was attempting to remove some of the paint from me when Grandpa walked into the kitchen. "For the love of Jezebel, boy! What's the matter with you? Do you know …"

Grandma interrupted. "Now, Al, calm down. He's only a boy."

Grandpa looked right at me. "I'll talk to you later. Right now we're going to try and catch that other cow. Charlie and I already have two of them tied up at Henry's. Come on. Let's go."

Years later, that grand old man was still telling the story of the day his grandson painted the animals green.

For punishment, Grandpa decided that I could not stay at the farm for the rest of the summer. I went to sleep crying.

The following day, fate intervened for me. I had put my suitcases in the old truck and decided that I would say a last goodbye to the old workhorse. Doll was still covered with green paint, and she was very quiet as I walked into the stall behind her. A halter had dropped from its peg on the bar wall, and as I leaned over to pick it up, I felt her hard, sharp horseshoes dig into my sitting part. The huge feet hurtled me toward the wall. That was all I remembered.

I awoke in the hospital, my head and the bottom part of me covered with bandages. Mom, Grandma, Grandpa, Uncle Charlie and some other relatives were standing around my bed. As I gazed around, my eyes focused on Grandpa.

"Grandpa … I'm sorry. I didn't mean to …"

Grandpa smiled. "Hush, boy. You just hurry up and get mended so you can get back out there on the farm for the rest of the summer."

The words were music, and I knew that everything was all right again. And it was.

Years later, and quite by chance, I met the pilot of the plane that had almost crashed on Grandfather's farm. He had descended low over the pasture to investigate what he thought was a green cow. Imagine! ❖

—Originally published in September 1976.

Mamma's Hands

By Adeline Roseberg

I think the Bicentennial Year gave us a new respect for our pioneer ancestors, and how they managed to make a life and a living for themselves, and how much they used their hands—something we are all having to do more of these days. Many of the younger generation choose to work with their hands both for a living and for creative pleasure and satisfaction.

Whenever I think of Mamma, I remember her hands. You'd expect that a pioneer mother of seven daughters and four sons, who worked hard under trying conditions, would have rough, red hands, but not Mamma! Mamma's hand were beautiful—narrow, with slender fingers, and soft skin, even though she used no creams or lotions. They were not delicate hands, but they were beautiful, and not only beautiful to look at, but supple, quick hands that were never idle!

She used to comb her long brown hair, bending at the waist as she combed downward, her hair almost touching the floor. Then she would stand up straight, and her hands would deftly twist all that hair into a neat pug on top of her head, sticking in a big bone hairpin here and there to keep it in place. We never tired of watching her do this, and you can be sure we saw it many times, as she always wore her hair in the same style.

> *I can see her strong hands rubbing clothes on the old washboard.*

I also remember how handily and gently she diapered a baby on her lap. There was always a new baby to care for. She'd hang onto baby with one hand, and with the other, spread a flannel triangle under the little bottom and dust it with talcum powder. Then, somehow, she always got those three safety pins just right. That, too, was always fascinating to watch.

Lovingly and tenderly, Mamma's hands wiped away our childish tears when we were hurt, and gave us an encouraging pat on the back if we did well on a job she had given us to do. There were so many of us, but she still found time for each one.

I remember our Saturday-night baths. She'd dip warm water out of the reservoir into a washtub on the kitchen floor by the wood stove. Mamma's hands had to help so many little bodies bathe before she could finally have her own bath, after we were clean and tucked into bed.

Mama's hands really flew on Sunday mornings, when we were getting ready for Sunday school. As we dressed around the heater in the dining room, she quickly found clean clothes for each one, tying shoelaces, buttoning dresses and combing hair.

I can see her strong hands rubbing clothes on the old washboard, in the kitchen during the winter and under a shade tree in summer.

As we got bigger, we all took our turns at the washboard, but there were many years when she did it alone. And how beautifully and capably her hands would iron the clothes with the old flatirons heated on the wood stove.

Her hands could wield a scrub brush, too, on a board floor, especially in the old summer kitchen. In summers, we cooked and ate in a separate little building to keep the big house from getting too hot and dirty from the fire used for cooking and canning. On her hands and knees, she would scrub one little square at a time, rubbing the brush occasionally on a big bar of soap, then scrubbing with vigor, and taking pride in each clean patch.

Mamma's hands did a wonderful job in the garden—planting, weeding, hoeing and picking, and then cooking and canning—so that many hungry mouths could be fed. Picking wild berries was her delight, especially blueberries. Her lively fingers could fill a bucket much more quickly than any of the rest of us could. We never could get as enthusiastic about picking as she did, but we were more than willing to eat her delicious, home-canned blueberry sauce, which was so good on waffles on a wintry day.

And what a job it was to make enough waffles to feed our hungry crew! The black, round waffle iron fit over an opening in the kitchen stove where a lid was removed. The heat had to be just right, and when the waffle was done on one side, the iron had to be flipped so that it could cook on the other side. Mamma's hands could do that just so. Waffles were a special treat, served once in a great while, and then for supper, not breakfast.

But Mamma often fried pancakes for us for breakfast on a long griddle that held eight pancakes at a time. Her hands stayed busy turning pancakes and frying side pork to go with them.

And her hands did a great job kneading her famous rye bread in the big dishpan. We were happy when she rolled out a flat bread, poked holes in it with a fork after it had raised a bit, and baked it first; we got to eat it hot out of the oven. Her hands were handy, too, at cutting

and baking big molasses cookies. They tasted so good to us with glasses of cold milk.

I can see Mamma with a coffee cup in her hands. A pause for a cup of coffee was her greatest luxury, and how she relished that first cup of coffee in the morning. Papa brought it

for her to drink before she got out of bed. A cup of coffee also helped celebrate happy events, cheered one when sad or troubled, and helped one relax. In Mamma's hands, a cup of coffee served many purposes.

And how quick she was to serve coffee to others, as when Papa brought customers in from his general store to share a cup of coffee and a bite to eat. Her nimble fingers had some food on the table in no time, and had poured up cups of the ever-ready coffee.

Visiting ministers always stayed at our house. Here, too, her hands were quick to serve, giving to each the best we had—the best sheets, the best towels, the best food.

Her capable hands could milk cows, too, and feed calves, and gather eggs, and rake the lawn, and do whatever had to be done.

Even when Mamma sat down to rest, her hands were forever busy.

Knitting was her relaxation—mittens and stockings to keep us warm, and a bit of crocheting and embroidering now and then to have some pretty things around. There were always overalls to patch, sometimes by lamplight far into the night if they were needed the next day.

In her spare time, she braided or crocheted rugs for the floors, and when we girls were little, she sewed dresses for us on the old treadle sewing machine. It was important for us all to have new dresses for such special occasions as the Sunday school and country school Christmas programs. The leftover scraps she used for patchwork quilts. Nothing was wasted.

I especially remember the beautiful velvet quilt she made with such painstaking care. One of Mamma's sisters had a hat store in town, and she gave Mamma boxes of velvet scraps, rich and colorful, from which she made a crazy quilt of pieces of all sizes and colors. Around each piece she worked fancy stitching with embroidery thread in contrasting colors to set off each piece.

This particular bit of handiwork was greatly admired by friends and neighbors. Not everyone had a velvet quilt. Mamma put it on the old sofa in the living room just for special occasions. To us, that velvet quilt was the height of elegance.

Mamma's hands had "green thumbs," too. Her houseplants always thrived. How carefully and faithfully she watered and tended them, and what joy they brought to her and everybody during the long, cold winters.

But above all, Mamma's hands were praying hands! Is it any wonder that when I think of Mamma, I especially remember her hands? ❖

—Originally published in May 1977.

Erick and Mary Swanson with their six eldest children in Glory, Minn. Three more daughters and two more sons were born later. The author is the little girl in the center front, between her Mamma and Papa.

A Girl Named Threedna?

By Carl W. Maiwald

I don't suppose any of you ever heard of a girl named Threedna, and neither have I, but my sister was almost stuck with that name by accident. The three people who were drawing names from Papa's best derby hat on that cold winter day in 1915 each had a different name in mind, but by a simple misunderstanding, my sister could have had one of the oddest names in the United States.

When I was born, I was named Carl William Maiwald, exactly like my father's older brother. When my brother came along, he was named Otto, after Mom's older brother. Everyone approved, especially my two uncles, but when my mother was expecting a girl—don't ask me how she could tell—a problem arose. Pop's sister was named Annie, the same as my mother, so he was in favor of calling the baby Annie, as that was a very popular name in those days.

"Virginia! That's not a girl's name; that's a state," Pop protested.

"Over my dead body," snapped my mother, stamping her small foot in defiance. "I don't want to be called 'Big Annie' and have the child called 'Little Annie,' even when she's a head taller than I am." As Mom was only 4 feet 11 inches tall, had an 18 inch waist (normally) and weighed a mere 98 pounds, the notion of calling her "Big Annie" did seem a bit ridiculous.

"Well, then, how about calling her Adeline? You know, like in the song *Sweet Adeline, My Adeline?*" Pop sang a few bars, his hearty baritone making the name sound pretty nice.

But Mom remembered when a quartet of drunken sailors had broken up a picnic by singing a ribald version of that song. "Not that name. Every time four bums who think they are Enrico Caruso get together, bellies full of beer and mustaches dripping foam, they sing 'Addooline,' sounding like lovesick tomcats. I think I'll call her Virginia."

"Virginia! That's not a girl's name; that's a state," Pop protested. "Might as well call her Rhode Island!

"Now Annie," said Pop hastily, as he detected a chill in the air, "remember, don't try to lift the coal pail when you take care of the fire. Just shovel a little out at a time. I have to go to work, and the fire isn't burned up enough to add coal yet. No heavy lifting; remember what Dr. LeLand said."

But I guess Mom did forget.

We lived in a nice, new, three-family house only half a block from the huge silk mill where Pop worked the night shift, 6 p.m. to 6 a.m. It was the Royal Weaving Company, the biggest silk mill in the world. Its red brick buildings, where looms clattered endlessly, stretched block after block along one side of the street.

In the rear was the maze of railroad tracks that kept this giant supplied with trainloads of soft coal to feed the boilers that powered its electric generators. In addition, the railroad brought the raw silk that had made the long voyage from China to New York Harbor. Back to New York, in the same cars, went millions of yards of dress goods. There, under the busy

fingers of women in sweatshops, the fabric became beautiful dresses.

The mill's mighty steam whistle, which blew at every shift change, would curl your toes. No one complained; it was nice to have something to set your Big Ben by.

When my father got home at 6:15 a.m. on that bitterly cold morning of Jan. 13, he was surprised when Briget, our washerwoman, met him at the door. Now, she was a sight to startle you anyway, because she had only a scattering of yellow teeth that showed up when a grin split her big red face. A wart on her potato-size nose and a few black hairs sprouting from a mole on her chin did nothing to dispel the image cast by her massive bulk and straggly hair.

Pop, who knew she was a sweet, kind person under that ugly exterior, wasn't bothered by her looks, only by her presence. "Is-is Annie all right?" he asked anxiously.

"She's just fine, and so is your new daughter. Come warm yourself by the stove so's you won't chill them. Your missus got caught with the pains so sudden, there wasn't time to call the doctor, 'cause he's over 80 and needs his sleep. Mrs. Morrison upstairs sent her Danny after me. If them kitchen scales are right, the baby is just 7½ pounds. One o'clock this morning is the time."

After Pop had properly kissed mother and daughter, Briget got out his fancy mustache coffee cup, put a big spoonful of sticky condensed milk in it, and poured coffee from the big gray enamel coffeepot that was always warming on the back of the old kitchen range. Then she got a cup for herself.

My father nearly choked on his first swallow of coffee when Briget remarked, "Such a nice name, Virginia."

Adam's apple bobbing nervously, he asked, "She isn't named yet, is she?"

"No, but Mrs. Morrison said she'd call the doctor from the grocery store, so I 'spect he'll get here this afternoon. It'll be up to him to make out the papers for City Hall."

"Virginia, West Virginia, North Carolina, South Carolina, Massachusetts."

"What on earth?"

"Geography. Sorry. Come along, Briget. We have to talk to Mrs. Maiwald before she falls back to sleep," said Pop, pushing back his almost untouched coffee.

My mother was breastfeeding the tiny, red newcomer as my dad asked anxiously, "You aren't going to call her Virginia, are you?"

"I most certainly won't name her Adeline."

"I'll tell you what, Annie, suppose we each write the name we choose on a slip of paper and put them in a hat. We'll let Briget pick one. Agreed?"

"Oh, all right, if you promise not to write Adeline on your slip."

"I promise on the condition you don't write Virginia on yours."

So it was agreed. In the cozy bedroom off the kitchen, which, unlike most bedrooms of the times, had a steam radiator, wallpaper with apple trees in bloom and two gas jets for light instead of only one, the drawing took place.

Pop got a writing pad, jotted a name, then folded it and dropped it into his best derby hat. Then he turned his back like a gentleman while Briget held a food tray so my mother could write a name on the pad. When that slip had been put into the hat, Mom sprung a surprise. "It's your turn now, Briget. Pick a nice name for the baby; you've earned the chance."

My father's mustache quivered with indignation, but he said nothing. Perhaps Lady Luck would smile on him.

Briget's big moon face got redder as she protested. "I don't, I, ah … can't … I … oh, all right." Taking a death grip on the pencil with one rough hand and on the table with the other, she went to the nightstand and wrote with grim concentration.

"She kept wetting the pencil with her tongue," said my father when he told me about it later. "I couldn't see what she wrote, but it seemed as if it had a hundred letters in it from the time it took. We didn't realize that Briget had never been to school and always signed her name with an X."

Pop shuffled the three slips and asked Mom to draw one. Awkwardly, for she was still nursing the baby, she selected one and handed it to my father. He unfolded it, then glared at Briget, saying, "Thank you. I hope my child will be happy with the name." He laid the paper on the bureau, put his hat in the closet and stamped out of the room.

In the kitchen, he dropped the two other slips into the stove before drinking his cold coffee and going to bed without his usual bowl of oatmeal. "*Threedna!* Holy mackerel! I should have let her name the baby Virginia!" he muttered as he dropped off to sleep.

When my dad woke up in the late afternoon, Briget had cooked a big pot of mutton stew for his supper. She'd baked bread and pie for his lunch pail, so he was in a slightly better mood. Mother and baby were napping, so after fortifying himself with a hearty meal, Pop questioned Briget. "Has the doctor been here yet?"

"That he has, Mr. Maiwald, and he says your wife and daughter are doing fine. The tyke is …"

"Harrumph! Did he make out the birth certificate?"

"Oh sure, like he always does. It's the law, he says."

"Well, what did he think of the fancy name? I bet he never heard *that* one before."

"Oh, he's heard it before. He said he was glad it wasn't something like Sophronziba or Scholastica, which is what his wife named their two daughters. Nope, he said Edna is short and sweet, just like the baby."

Edna! So "3dna" was "Edna," not "Threedna," Pop realized. He'd thought Briget had been using a sort of shorthand; instead, she had gotten the E turned around. Edna … not bad. Nobody we knew had it; there would be no jealousies in the family.

"That's a great name, Briget," he smiled. "You must have picked it because it reminds you of a dear friend."

Briget's broken teeth showed in a happy grin. "To tell the truth, Mr. Maiwald, it's the only name I figured I could spell." ❖

—Originally published in January 1978.

Mr. Pettigrew and The Toothbrush

By Mary Alice Hunt

One day Papa came home from the farm and found Mama sitting at the table, pencil in hand and page after page of figures before her. "What in the world are you doing?" Papa asked.

"I've decided on a way that I can bring in a few nickels and boost our budget some," Mama said.

"Sounds interesting," Papa nodded, "but how do you plan to do it?"

Mama said, "You know train connections are bad, and it would be a real service to the drummers who come here to work the surrounding territory if they had someplace to stay while they are working the little towns around here. They could rent a rig from the livery stable, work several little towns in one day, and make it back to Conroe for the night, so you see, it would help them and us, too."

Anybody with any sense at all could tell that I was a girl.

"Well, we do have plenty of room, and it does sound logical." Papa studied for a minute. "It would mean an awful lot of extra work for you. Are you sure you want to do this?"

"I've thought about all that and I'm sure." Mama always knew exactly what she wanted, so the next week Mama hung out her sign and the drummers began to come.

There was one I never did like. He was Mr. Pettigrew. Every time he saw me, he'd say, "Hello, little boy!" That always made me furious. Anybody with any sense at all could look at my pigtails and my dress and tell that I was a girl.

Hilda and I were just children, but we liked to hang around and listen to the drummers exchange jokes. Sometimes some mighty funny things happened.

One morning, Papa was in the kitchen, drying dishes for Mama. He was downright mad when he looked out the kitchen window and saw what Mr. Pettigrew was doing.

"Looka there, Floy!" That was Mama's name. "If that dang drummer is not out there using *my* toothbrush!"

He pointed his finger at the dapper young man on the back porch, who, having given his teeth the final brush, was preening before the mirror over the wash shelf. He slicked down his hair and straightened his bow tie. He was a dandy—his vest and spats told you that.

Papa's ruddy face was even redder as he stamped his foot. "This is the last straw!" he exclaimed. "I've put up with that drummer polishing his shoes with the last bit of polish I had, and I even overlooked his coming in to breakfast late and making extra work for you, Floy—but this is just too much!"

Papa stomped up and down the kitchen floor, clenching and unclenching his big fists and muttering under his breath. "I'll teach that d— Pettigrew a lesson if it is the last thing I do!" The color in his face made his blue eyes look black. Papa didn't often swear, so we knew he was pretty upset.

Before long, a look came over his face and a gleam came in his eye. I knew then that he had a plan, but I didn't know what it was till later.

After meals, the traveling men who stayed at our house had the habit of congregating on the cool back porch to enjoy a visit with one another before they scattered and went about their own business.

One particular morning, not long after Papa saw Mr. Pettigrew using his toothbrush, I came

around the house with old Max, the bird dog. All the drummers and Papa had already congregated on the porch for their morning chat.

Papa had a mysterious look on his face like he knew something he was not supposed to tell. He called the dog, "Come here, Max!"

Max ran up to him, wagging his tail and slobbering. He didn't know what was in store for him. Papa patted him on the head with one hand and reached up on the wash shelf with the other and got his toothbrush. "It's time we brushed your gums, old boy," he told Max—and he began brushing the dog's teeth.

"Papa, why—" I started to interrupt, but a straight look and a shake of his head stopped me cold.

Old Max was howling and raising the devil every way he knew how, and Papa was dancing around, trying to hold him and brush his teeth at the same time. The commotion went on for what seemed like a long time.

I opened my mouth and interrupted, again. "I thought the vet said—" Again, Papa stopped me with a hard stare, and went right on scrubbing the dog's gums.

His job done, Papa put the toothbrush back on the shelf. He turned to the drummers and explained, "Old Max is a fine bird dog, but he has a bad gum disease, and the vet told me to brush his gums every day, so I keep this toothbrush out here handy to use on him."

Mr. Pettigrew didn't say a word, but I noticed his face turned pale and he looked sort of scared. He rushed into the house, and when he came back a few minutes later, there was the strong smell of disinfectant about him.

But do you know, as long as Mr. Pettigrew worked this territory, he never again was caught using Papa's toothbrush. ❖

—*Originally published in March 1978.*

Forget-Me-Not Hat

By Holly Gauer

Mother had insisted on remaining in our old home after Father had died. Now that she was alone, I tried to visit her more often. Every room in that house was dearly familiar to me, but it had been many years since I had been in the attic. This day I was helping Mother wrap a birthday gift for Aunt Kate, and there was plenty of ribbon, Mother said, in a Christmas box she kept at the head of the attic stairs.

I had forgotten how narrow those stairs were, how steep the creaking steps. A single dusty bulb hung from the electric cord. I reached up to it to turn the switch on and sent the dim light swinging. Pocketing the desired ribbon, I stood for a moment to look around at this forgotten yet well-remembered room. The moving bulb scattered shadows, its light picking out objects, each dust-covered with sentiment.

A small round hatbox captured my attention. Its color was indistinguishable, as was the silken cord that was still attached.

I don't know why I tiptoed, but I did. Gently I lifted the brittle lid and turned back the yellowed tissue paper.

As I peeked into the box, I heard again my brother's high-pitched chant:

It was her weakness that made her sin;
Her weakness for hats that did her in. …

As if it had been packed tight in that box, the past exploded, flooding my mind, all the details explicitly remembered.

I was 9 years old and had been to the new 5-and-10 to buy a nickel's worth of candy. The remaining 20 cents were tied in a knot in my handkerchief, secure in my pocket, saved for the children's Saturday afternoon picture show.

I was passing the millinery store when the hat stopped me. It was true—I'd had a weakness for hats since I was a toddler, parading around in anyone's hat I could get my hands on, including unwarned visitors.

This hat was displayed front and center in the millinery store showcase: a creamy Milan straw bonnet, its crown wreathed with blue velvet forget-me-nots lying in pale pink netting. Trailing black velvet ribbons tied a bow under the mannequin's chin.

That the hat would fit me was probable. That it was made for me, I had no doubt. That this most beautiful hat in the world should be mine, there was no question. How to get it—that was something else.

I figured my allowance—25 cents a week. Two quarters made 50 cents. Two 50 cents made $1 … four weeks … one month—and the sign in front of the hat was marked $12. I counted the months on my fingers. I was already near the end of May. A whole year! That was forever. No use asking my parents. Father had bought Sally and me spring hats barely two weeks ago.

I jerked myself away from the window, but at the corner, I stopped, turned and went back to the millinery store. It had occurred to me that I might charge the hat to my father. I had shopped with Mother and heard her say many times, "Charge it, please, to Mr. Adolph Zimmerman," and we walked out of the store with the purchase, not paying a cent. One little ping of doubt bothered me: Mother was an adult, and I was not. At least, I decided after gazing at the bonnet, I could go into the store and try the hat on. I felt sure Miss Nettie would let me do that, and maybe it wouldn't fit my head.

But it did. I carefully tied the bow. The streamers came almost to my waist. My blond curls fell forward. The blue forget-me-nots matched my eyes, which suddenly filled with stars. It was astonishing. I looked like somebody else—a child movie star probably, I thought, and I walked straight over to Miss Nettie.

"I'll take this hat," I said, "and charge it to my father please, Mr. Adolph Zimmerman."

I remember the startled look on the milliner's face. "But this hat is $12, Holly. I don't think your father would be pleased," she said.

I looked her squarely in the eye and found out how amazingly easy I could lie. "He saw it in the window himself," I said, "so I reckon he knows the price. You see, it's for my birthday. My father said for me to charge it, Miss Nettie."

She hesitated for a long moment while I held my breath. Then she smiled and said, "Well, in that case, happy birthday." And she wrote out the sales slip. Then she turned to a shelf and lifted down a pale blue round box.

I asked, in a whisper, "What's that for?"

"Your new hat."

Any hat I'd ever had before came in a sack. My amazement must have been apparent. She said, "Our hats have boxes. You keep them nicer in their own box, and you can wear them longer." Later, I wondered if Miss Nettie was one of those people who could see into the future.

I adored the round box with its blue silk cord, but I wasn't ready to take off my bonnet. To think it was mine made me slightly dizzy. "I'll wear the hat," I said, "and carry the box."

Miss Nettie tucked the sales slip into the tissue-lined box and handed it to me. "Well, you do look pretty as a picture in your new hat, and it is your birthday." She smiled.

Floating home, I was bothered by one thing—my sins. I counted three—three lies. I couldn't remember telling a lie before. Would God forgive me? Could sinners go to church? I sang in the children's choir and loved to sing.

I encountered Father first. My new hat did not go unnoticed. Mother was called in. With each question and answer, Father's outrage mounted. No one escaped. Certainly not the milliner. No one but *no one* in our family was ever to purchase a hat from Nettie Clark again. The fact that she had accepted the charge of a $12 hat to a child made her a greedy accomplice.

That I had lied to her did not excuse her. She knew Father would be in his grocery store. She could have phoned. Besides, he had just bought hats for his two daughters, and she, Nettie Clark, being an adult and the only milliner in town, knew that he, Adolph Zimmerman, never spent more than $5 on *anyone's* hat, and that included himself and Mother. We waited until the after-Easter sales and Nettie Clark *knew* it.

Mother said quietly, "Holly will be punished and the hat returned." She studied me for a moment and added, "Pity, though."

Tearfully I offered to pay for my hat with my quarter-a-week allowance, but I was interrupted by Father. "I will make the decisions in this household!" he thundered. Then, looking away from me, he lowered his voice. "Honesty is not bought, Holly Zimmerman. Go to your room. I will call you."

Shivering, I perched myself on the high four-poster, not daring even to swing my legs. I was the petted baby of the family. I had never been spanked, never been scolded like this—but neither had I ever lied about my father.

My parents' room adjoined mine. My door was ajar and so was theirs.

It was her weakness that made her sin; her weakness for hats that did her in.

I could hear their voices. Father's was a loud whisper, "Edith, when that child walked in the door, her eyes like blue stars and the flowers matching them, that bow tied under her chin—I tell you, Edith, my daughter looked like an angel." Then he moaned, "Edith, how can your daughter look like an angel and do a thing like this? Twelve dollars!"

That I was eavesdropping did not occur to me. I simply slipped to my door so I could hear better. The mention of money often caused my father to moan—but this money concerned me.

Mother cautioned, "Adolph, don't have a heart attack. I admit Holly did not ask your permission, took authority into her own hands, and also lied, terribly—but for the first time, Adolph, and she has been with me when I have charged things."

Still Father moaned. "To think I bought the girls hats just two weeks ago—I picked them out myself!"

"I know," Mother said, "three weeks after Easter. That each hat was reduced to $1.98 and Holly's was two sizes too large for her is, of course, beside the point."

"I told you to line her hatband with paper," Father said.

"I did," Mother said sweetly, "and by flattening her ears, she manages to hold it up. Holly is 9, Adolph. She is female, and perhaps she takes after her mother."

There was silence. I hastily hopped back onto my bed, every word of that adult conversation indelibly inscribed on my brain, to be re-examined and better understood with the passage of time.

After a few moments, I was summoned into the parlor and stood facing the semicircle of my family—my older brother, mother, father and my older sister. It was explained to me that charging *anything* without the permission of the person paying for it was the same as stealing—in this case, stealing from my own father. It was a sin, certainly—"Thou shalt not steal."

Also, I had told three lies—three more sins against my father. "Thou shalt not bear false witness." I had broken two commandments.

In my sorry mind, the church, the choir, faded from my life. I stood there, the accused, confused, and confessed the stolen goods still on my head.

"Holly Zimmerman," my father's voice commanded, and I lifted my tear-filled eyes to his. He wiped his brow, and also, to my astonishment, his eyes. There was no anger in his voice when he spoke, but it was firm and clear.

"You will wash and dry the dinner dishes, unassisted, for three weeks, 21 days. You shall attend no parties whatsoever, nor the Saturday afternoon picture shows for one month—31 days. You will neither own nor wear any other hat than the one on your head for three successive years—other than a toboggan cap in the winter—and I trust you will ask forgiveness of the Lord for your sins. Holly, do you hear me?"

"Yes, sir," I answered meekly. Then, wishing to express my sincerity, I searched for passages from the Bible, but Robin Hood was better remembered. I began bravely, "I heard you, sir, and shamefully accept my just fate. I am sorry to the heart I stole from you, dear Daddy, sir." At this point, I dissolved completely into tears.

My father waved his arms frantically and cried, "Edith, Edith, do something!"

Mother led me from the room and told me I would start my penance the next day. Tonight I would eat supper in my room.

The weeks, the months, the three years passed. I grew up quickly, and that third summer, my Milan hat sat a little too high on my head, but there was no complaint from me. Perhaps I should have hated that hat with the forget-me-nots, but I never did, and when I gave it to the church for the rummage sale (as we did with articles that were no longer useful to us), I felt a kind of sadness and loss. I even experienced some sense of indignation when I saw it tossed on the 5-cent table—until I saw my own dad buy it back.

My thoughts returned to the attic, and with a smile and a tear, I dusted the box with my apron, arranged the yellowed tissue and replaced the lid.

Before turning off the attic light, I glanced again at the small, faded blue box where I knew Father had placed it, near the trunk holding Mother's wedding dress and Sally's one-legged doll. ❖

—Originally published in March 1978.

She Outshines Them All

By Len Colp

My mom was not just your average run-of-the mill woman. Fact is, she was not even your regular type of farm woman. I suppose that is what made her special to Dad and me. I mean, even before that fall. It was September. The wheat stood tall and golden in the field back of the barn. The old harvest sun poured out gallons and gallons of hot golden rays from a clear blue sky. Someone had pulled a plug on the giant fan that blew a breeze. In the autumn heat, the wind would have been welcomed with open arms.

Time was overripe for harvest to begin. Father was late this year, for he was still making repairs to the binder when he should have been in the field. He and I had spent the morning changing the bull wheel. It was slow, heavy work. The truth was, we still didn't have it finished when Mom called us for dinner.

Mom dropped the dishcloth and helped Father into the closest chair.

After dinner, Father said to me, "You can help your mother with the dishes." Then he pushed his chair back from the table.

"I'd rather help you," I protested.

"Mom first," he answered as he put on his cap.

"Jake," Mom stopped him as he reached for the screen door. "I need a bit of wood to finish up baking bread. Do you think you could split an armful or two before you get started again? Len will bring it up."

"Yup," Father answered as he passed over the threshold. The door closed behind him.

Five minutes later the door opened and Father limped through it. His face was white, its muscles twisted and knotted in pain.

"What's wrong?" Concern leaped from Mom's heart as she turned and saw the look on his face.

"I cut my foot."

Both Mom and I stared at the 4-inch cut in the toe of Father's work boot. Blood was already visible through the crack.

Mom dropped the dishcloth and helped Father into the closest chair, where he removed his boot. As he dropped it beside the chair, a small pool of blood emerged from it. When he removed his sock, more blood gushed out of a gaping 3-inch hole in his foot.

"Get the cornstarch," Mom ordered me.

I took it from the cupboard and she sprinkled it into the wound until at last, most of the bleeding had stopped. As she rose to her feet, she said to me, "Len, forget the dishes. Get some towels from the linen closet and put them in the buggy. We have to take your father into Dr. Sawyer's."

"No you ain't," Father said in his uneducated way, but as he stood up, the blood broke through the cornstarch again. The pain caused him to sit back down immediately. "I'm not going in there. I ain't got no $3 to fatten Sawyer's bank account with."

"Take the cornstarch with you," Mom said, as I started toward the linen closet; then she answered Father. "Suit yourself. It's either $3 for Dr. Sawyer or $100 for Mr. McDuff."

McDuff was the undertaker.

Mom pulled off her apron and followed me outside. She ran to the barn, and by the time I came out of the shop where we kept the buggy, she was already coming with Bell and Nancy; they were harnessed and ready to hitch to the buggy. When we had them hooked up, she took Bell by the bridle and led them to the back door.

"Hold them here, Len," she ordered as she ran inside.

"Pansy, I ain't going!" Father complained as he and Mom came out on the back steps. He was hobbling on one foot as Mom supported him, his arm around her neck. But even as he protested, he did his part in getting to the buggy.

Mom never answered him. They came down the steps together and over to the buggy. Father struggled into it. Mom and I slid into the seat beside him. She took the reins from the line pole and tapped Bell and Nancy lightly on their backs. The two of them broke into a fast trot.

It took us a couple of hours to cover the 16 miles to town. By the time we arrived at the

doctor's office, Father's foot had swollen, and the cornstarch was red and dried and cracked.

Dr. Sawyer ushered him in at once. By now Father was quiet, but when he came out of the examination room, he was back on the protest march, even if he could only walk on one foot.

"Doctor," he protested, "I am a farmer, and it's harvesttime. I can't be sitting around nursing this foot. I got work to do!" He spoke as if it were Dr. Sawyer's fault that he had cut his foot.

"I know you are busy, but you had better be looking after that foot or I'll be hospitalizing you," Dr. Sawyer answered as he handed Father a set of crutches. That ended the argument.

When we got back into the buggy and Bell and Nancy had started for home, Father sat with his foot propped up on the dashboard. He was very quiet. I didn't know if he was silent because of the pain or because of he was worried about the crop. When we arrived home, he got out of the buggy without a word and crutched himself into the house. Mom and I put the horses in the barn. Then she said, "You'd better run for the cows, Len."

It was past milking time by now. A half-hour later the cows entered the barnyard. As they did so, Mom came from the milk shed with a bucket and a milk stool. She lined up old Earla first and sat down and began to milk. There were 10 more to go. Supper came late that night, but Mom had the chores done.

"I wish we could afford a hired man," Father said as he pushed back from the table.

"Don't worry about it," Mom said.

Father half-grinned at Mom as he said, "I don't know how you and Sawyer expect me to get that crop off. I mean with you both ganging up on me this way."

"We'll manage," Mom comforted him as she took her hands out of the dishwater. "We've seen hard times before, Jake, and the Lord has never let us starve. He isn't about to start now."

"I suppose you're right, but I always kind of think this place depends on me." Father lifted his right leg with both hands and set it down gently as he turned from the table.

Mom dumped the dishwater into the pail by the door before she answered. "That's human, though I can't say it's right."

Next day, Uncle Joe dropped by. He had not heard about Father's accident. He had just come for a minute, but he stayed to fix the binder. It took him an hour to finish.

"She's ready," Uncle Joe said to Mom as he wiped the grease from his hands. "The only one problem is you still don't have a driver. When I get finished at home, I'll see what I can do if you still need help then."

"Don't worry about it," Mom answered. "We'll get it in before the snow flies."

"Now that you got the binder fixed, I'll be at it tomorrow," Father said. "I'm a-figurin' I can use the other foot to trip the bundle carrier."

Mom didn't answer him, but Uncle Joe did. "If you can manage that way, you can send Len for me if you have a breakdown."

That hot afternoon Mom saddled Dixie to ride off to the back pasture to bring in Doll and Bob. We would need two more horses to help Bell and Nancy pull the binder. Mom went in spite of Father's protests.

"It's not a woman's job," he reasoned. "I can ride because I'll not be using my foot."

Mom only smiled and answered, "You'd get chasing the horses through the bush and bang that foot, then you'd end up in the hospital." With that she rode away. In spite of the fact that he had argued with her, he knew she was right.

By 8 the next morning, Mom had our 11 cows milked and turned out into the pasture. She also had the cream separated from the milk. When Father came out of the house, she had just finished hitching the horses to the binder.

He climbed up into the seat and settled himself like a king on a throne.

"You don't be using that right foot," Mom cautioned as he slid his left foot into the saddle of the bundle carrier trip mechanism.

He tripped the carrier and set it back in position before he answered, "I'll manage," then he added, "I told you I could do it." I thought he was reassuring himself more than Mom.

"You're sure you'll be OK?" Mom worried.

"I'll be fine," he answered as he took the reins from her. He spoke to the horses, and they moved off toward the field. Then I heard Mom pray, "Lord, watch over my man. We can't get the crop in without Your help. Thank You in advance, Lord. I know You're watching over us."

Every hour the horses and the binder and Father came around the field and were within sight of the kitchen window. And Mom was there every hour to check, or worry if they were a second late.

At noon she met Father and unhitched the horses to put them in the barn. Each stall had already had its ration of oats and hay laid out. After dinner, she got them ready again. She never complained about her added chores, nor did Father grumble about the pain in his foot.

Day after day, Mom harnessed and hitched the horses to the binder. Father drove them.

Mom began the stooking, for she knew that Father could never walk the miles required to stook 200 acres of wheat. I helped her, or perhaps I only got in the way. Anyway, I was 3.

By thrashing time, Father was off the crutches, but when he mentioned thrashing, Dr. Sawyer shook his head. "No, Jake, I can't honestly say that you're fit for that kind of work. Truthfully, you'd be pushing that foot too far."

It was Fred Waters who came to our rescue.

"Look, Jake," he said in his quiet way, "we're not going to see you stuck. If you think you can handle the tractor and the separator, I'll run your team." Fred owned the outfit, and he thrashed for Father every year.

By the time the snow flew late that October, the wheat was in. As the last thrashing wagon left our yard, I heard Mom say again, "Thank You, Lord. You always look after Your own."

Many is the time since then that I've heard Father say, "I must agree when the Bible says, 'Whosoever findeth a wife findeth a good thing and obtaineth favour of the Lord.' I got Pansy and she outshines them all! Praise the Lord for his goodness to this poor farmer!" ❖

—Originally published in September 1978.

Logging Camp Sugar Cookie

By Geva E. Ingram

A good cook was a priceless asset to a logging camp. A proficient cook who turned out tasty, filling meals could instantly transform poorly fed woodsmen—and therefore discontented and unproductive woodsmen—into a cheerful, hard-working timber-cutting crew. In 1920, Arnie cooked for the logging camp some 20 miles northeast of Sedro Woolley, Wash., where my widowed teamster father and I lived. Arnie was an artist with pots and pans, and as such, he was held in high regard. However, the loggers ragged him unceasingly; for example, they sang *Who Put the Overalls in Mrs. Murphy's Chowder?* while trooping to the sawbuck-and-plank tables. But they knew very well that he produced meals Fannie Farmer might have proudly served, and that he did it with a few simple ingredients and primitive kitchen equipment.

***Arnie took a deep breath
and called the loggers to breakfast.***

In my 6-year-old, little-girl way, I idolized Arnie. That he chewed cut-plug, had a scraggly handlebar mustache and habitually wore a flour-sack apron and a derby hat—"even to bed," the loggers vowed—was of small consequence. Didn't he patiently put up with my everlasting begging for snacks and save me spoons to lick and pans to scrape? In my adoring eyes, Arnie was a logging camp sugar cookie, and his culinary skills gave him all the glamour needed.

Cooking wasn't his only camp skill, however; his talent was "double-bitted." Since he got up at 3:30 a.m. to fire up the massive cast-iron cookstove, he was the camp's official alarm clock, too.

Arnie "rousted 'em out" at 5 a.m. with a minimum of the usual bunkhouse getting-up grousing. Although most camp cooks had a favorite get-up jingle—repeated morning after morning, it became their trademark—Arnie always varied and sometimes improvised his calls. "We wake ourselves up at a quarter to 5, just to be sure that we won't miss a new one," some of the loggers claimed.

When the pitch-knot fire was crackling in the huge range with its attached hot-water reservoir, it nearly blotted out the *Police Gazette*–papered rear wall. The slab bacon sliced, the pancake batter mixed and the great, oblong iron griddles popping grease, Arnie took a deep breath and called the loggers to breakfast.

Facing page: *Good Old Days* magazine cover, January 1979, House of White Birches nostalgia archives

His first call of the week might be "Rise and shine, you sleeping beauties!" The following morning, perhaps he'd yell, "Get up and get to swampin'! Are ya gonna lay there all day an' wear out the bunks?" Next day, he'd turn poet: "The griddle's hot and the bacon's hoppin'. Rise up, boys! Let's get choppin'!" Another call of his was "Come and get it, or I'll throw it to the hogs!" That one was inelegant, perhaps, but not far-fetched; camp cooks did indeed raise pigs.

Most logging camps of that era maintained a pigsty; hogs were the garbage disposal of the logging hinterlands. To us five kids living at the camp, though, those pigs proved to be a Jonah.

We kids ate at the cookhouse, after the loggers had finished their meal and gone to work. Swinging a double-bitted ax, pulling a crosscut saw or trimming shingle bolts for a 10-hour day gave the loggers prodigious appetites.

What *our* excuse was, I don't know, but we kids rivaled them as trenchermen; yet, no matter how we overstuffed ourselves at mealtime, sweets were our passion—especially Arnie's pies. And that fondness was our downfall.

We had become as adept at cadging goodies as road-seasoned bindle stiffs. Being the youngest of the camp kids, I was the most likely to sway Arnie's sympathies. And so I'd launch our daily campaign for handouts.

"Mmmm, Arnie, your pies smell good!" I'd say. "They look yummy, too. Did you make extra ones today?"

If flattery failed, we tried the pitiable, starving-kid routine: "We're so hungry, Arnie. How long is it till supper? … That long? … Well, could we just have a few cookies, maybe …?" Here, the knack that paid off in a snack was to let the voice trail off faintly, always indicating that famine was about to lay us low. We seldom went away empty-handed.

Once we wandered up the hillside above the camp, picking blueberries, and returned in midafternoon, long after the noon meal. Not having eaten since breakfast, we were hungry—*really*—and we headed for the cookhouse.

Cook, however, had suffered a rare kitchen disaster: overheated ovens and, as a result, overbrowned pies. His supper menu was short and his temper was the same. Neither big-eyed wiles nor pitiful pleas brought forth anything but a curt and peevish "You kids go outside, and don't you come back in here until suppertime."

Still grumbling, Arnie lay on the porch bench for a nap. Up since 3:30 a.m., he was entitled, but by so doing, he proved our undoing. Hunger won out over ethics. We sneaked to the rear of the cook shack, where the remaining unburned raisin pies were cooling on the windowsill, and made off with three of them.

Back of the nearby bunkhouse, in a brush-hidden, secluded corner, we divided and devoured the pies. Then—but only then—remorse set in. If we had confessed at this point, while our misdeed was yet a minor infraction, we'd have been scolded but forgiven.

As we saw it, the pigs would make a perfect scapegoat. So we sidled up to the pigsty, unlatched the gate and, using the empty but still syrupy pie pans for bait, lured the half-grown, innocent shoats towards the cook shack window. Once there, we dropped the pie tins to the ground and, as the hogs began rooting at them, yelled, "Arnie, come quick! The pigs are out!"

Only when the excitement of chasing four squealing, fleet-footed, freedom-happy porkers back into their pen had died down did a sharp-eyed amateur sleuth remark, "No half-grown pig could reach that 4-foot high windowsill, and even if one did, those pies would have fallen in, not out, and be laying on the kitchen floor now."

Alas, we were caught, sticky-raisin-fingered, in common thievery and a cover-up to boot.

At the supper table our disgrace was disclosed to all. Father's stern face promised punishment. (But do I remember a faint twitch at the corner of his mouth?) At any rate, except for mealtimes, the cookhouse was declared off limits, and all goody-begging forbidden—forever.

Conscience-stricken, lonely and miserable, I spent many hours through the next weeks sitting on a culled cedar log across the road from the cook shack, hoping that Arnie would come out and talk to me. He didn't, though. I suppose that Father had warned him that in my case, isolation was the proper corrective penalty.

Before long, however, an occasional cookie or doughnut was waiting on my penitent's log when I got there. Arnie, it appeared, didn't think of me as a completely lost soul. ❖

—Originally published in January 1979.

My Most Unforgettable Character

By Mary Ellen Stelling

My father was the gentlest and fairest man I ever knew. People took shameful advantage of this fairness and gentleness. In all the years I was privileged to know and love my father, I never heard him utter a complaining word, and yet many times I knew his heart was raw and bleeding. I have felt his hand tremble and seen the tears stand in his hazel eyes, but his chin was always up.

Life was demanding, and my father gave whatever it asked of him. He gave beyond his strength and his ability. He gave unstintingly of his services to family, business and community.

He was a very modest, almost reticent person. I don't believe he realized how many people loved him, for no one thought to tell him until it was too late. When he was no more, when he could not hear his praises sung, the people gathered to do him honor.

My father was a simple man who loved his home and his child.

Days after his passing, people unknown to the family called to tell of small favors he had done for them. At his funeral, people gathered outside his home. Many a strong working man stood unashamed with tears coursing down his cheeks.

My father was a simple man who loved his home and his child. He was the kind of man who should have had a family of six rosy, jolly children, but I was his only one, and, when I was 6 years old, my mother left him and took me with her. I was not old enough to fully realize what that meant to him. I only realized that I missed him and that we needed each other. Thereafter, I only saw him in the summer, when I was permitted to visit him at the home of my grandparents.

I was a strong-willed child. No one could do as much with me as he could, but I had an instinctive desire not to hurt him. When strong threats by other people failed to move me, my father had only to say, "Minty, I want you to do it," and it was done.

I remember him on the tennis courts and on the golf course in the summer twilight, and puttering about in his garden as the fireflies gathered in the grass. One time he told me to plant some lettuce seeds and the fairies would make them come up in my initials. Somewhat dubiously I planted the seeds and then was led away to bed. Sure enough, in the appointed time, there the lettuce lay, trim and neat, spelling out M.E.T. to my bedazzled eyes. My belief in fairies has been undaunted ever since.

He was never too tired to play with me, to read to me or to draw fascinating men on the edge of his favorite magazine for my amusement. In winter, he pulled me over the snowy hills on my little sled until he gasped for breath.

When I returned to him in the summer, little and lonely and longing for my mother's comforting hand at bedtime, my father would take me upstairs and we would undress, kneel together to pray, and then go to bed. Years later, I learned that after he had gotten me to sleep, he would arise and dress again and go back downstairs for the rest of the evening.

In winter, he pulled me over the snowy hills on my little sled until he gasped for breath.

He often worked late in the evening at the bank, and he would take my dog and me along to play in the dark corners of the deserted bank, or put me up on a telephone book at one of the typewriters to play while he bent over his desk, working on his ledgers. Then, afterward, we would have our ice-cream cones and walk up the hill to bed, hand in hand.

When I was far away at school in the winter, he never failed to send me gorgeous flowers, candy and toys on every holiday. On my mother's birthday, he sent me a check to buy her present. He never forgot me or how I needed him. Even when my mother remarried and had a baby boy, and I was full of enthusiastic talk about my little brother, my father became my most interested listener.

He encouraged me to write stories, and his wallet was always filled to overflowing with dog-eared scraps of my juvenile poems and pictures. At his death, these bits of worn and nearly threadbare papers were given to me, some of them almost 20 years old and practically illegible from constant handling.

We shared a bond that I find difficult to put into words. We were drawn closer together because we felt that we were the only ones in the world who really understood what the other felt. We knew, although we seldom mentioned it, that we shared a common loss—the home life we should have had together.

When the time for parting rolled around each fall, I would cling to him, weeping, protesting that I could not leave him. That is when I felt his hands tremble as he tore me from his coat lapels and sought to console me.

I have seen tears of anguish and pain stand in his eyes as he sought in a yearning, futile way to provide me with the sense of security which he knew I must carry with me into another winter without him.

So many pictures of him tumble into my mind that I find it hard to put them down in chronological order. I remember him escorting me to my first dance.

I was far too young and much too chubby to achieve even a semblance of popularity, but he sensed how terribly important it was to me, and so he valiantly waltzed me around and around the floor while I prayed that some youngster would ask me to dance.

I can close my eyes now and see us dancing—one, two, three, slowly and dignified, a tall, thin, dapper man with a little black mustache and his chubby little daughter in her flat silver slippers. He was a good dancer, and he loved to waltz.

In fact, he was an incurable romantic, but he was too shy to admit it even to himself, and so he tried to keep it frozen in behind a wall of implacable dignity. Sometimes it escaped and he gave vent to his feelings, but he was always ashamed of himself when he did.

There was something of the dreamer about him, and yet he had a keen, analytical mind. He came of Quaker stock, and his conscience and a strong sense of duty drove him. I think he could have been a gay, happy-go-lucky, charming person, but he felt he could not allow himself to be one. He waged a constant battle with himself, and duty always won. It drove him too hard and finished him before his time. I didn't realize until after his death, when the letters came pouring in, just how many chairmanships and other offices he had filled on various civic boards.

He was a very democratic man. He really loved people from all walks of life. He had a way with them, too. He was the one the "hunky" miners always called for in their broken English when they had banking business to transact. It was him they named guardian of their children when they died. At one time, he had 20 orphaned children under his care.

One day an Armenian pack peddler came into the bank and told my father how he had escaped from the Turks and come to this country. His wife had been murdered, and his two babies were somewhere in Armenia. I believe my father was drawn to this man because of their mutual longing for their children. At any rate, my father helped Fatim Magee bring his daughter to this country.

Another time, my father was traveling in Europe with two rather haughty friends. The first night out, upon entering the dining room, they found themselves seated at a table with a black man. Mr. and Mrs. Page were outraged and immediately demanded that their seats be changed. But my father refused to move, and he said later that he found his dark-complexioned dinner companion the most interesting conversationalist it had ever been his privilege to meet. They became firm friends, and my father learned that the man was a fabulously wealthy Indian prince, and an Oxford graduate.

When Mr. and Mrs. Page heard this, they regretted their hasty action and tried, to no avail, to be reseated at the prince's table. At the end of the voyage, the prince invited my father to bring me to visit him at one of his many palaces.

I remember my father standing and singing *Old Nassau*, the song of his alma mater, his cheeks pink with emotion. I remember him standing beside me in church and trying to keep in tune with some old hymn. I remember him taking me to dinner at the old Waldorf, with a large gardenia corsage pinned to my 11-year-old person.

There were so many things we were denied, and yet we found so many things to strengthen the bond between us and hold us close in spite of the intervening miles. We knew how important we were to each other without any need for maudlin sentimentality between us.

Now that he is gone, I find it hard to believe. His personality was, to me, so great, so strong, that I am sure he is very near me yet. Yes, he was my most unforgettable character. ❖

—Originally published in April 1979.

Mama and The Chicken Thief

By Mary L. Couch

Dad worked nights at the coal mine. This left Mama with her 11-year-old sister, Opal, who had been motherless since she was 2 years old, 3-year-old me, and our dog, Bess. Mama was awed at the rough life in a mining town, but loved the people, whose kindness could not be excelled anywhere. When Dad and Mama married, he brought her to this town surrounded by mountains. She mistook the mountains for clouds and expected a storm at any moment. It was a long time before she got over this idea.

Mama was a beautiful woman, with olive complexion, black hair and eyes so brown they were almost black. They snapped when she was angry. Dad was very proud of her. He bought her a pistol and taught her to shoot because there were snakes and other varmints around the cabin.

Dad called it "castle in a cabin" because love was there, although money was scarce. Dad and Mama built it for temporary housing until a nice house could be built. It had one long room with a folding bed and piano back to back for a partition. Another room that served as kitchen and dining room had flagstones for a floor, and was level with the ground, but the long room was perhaps 2 feet above the ground in the back and less in the front.

The cabin site in a secluded spot in thick woods was not far from neighbors. There was no telephone or electricity, and water had to be carried from half a mile away, except that which was saved in barrels and tubs when it rained. Our daily chore was to get a bucket and go for water. As often as not, when dusk began to fall and panthers squalled from the nearby mountains, I ended up being carried along with my little pail of water. Hospitality reigned. We had a lot of company. When we came home from church on Sunday, we often found a carload or wagonload of visitors waiting for us. Somehow, Mama always managed a good meal, and sometimes a night or two of lodging. Everyone might sleep on pallets, but no one seemed to mind. Mama never complained about inconveniences.

She raised chickens to help with the food bill. She managed to acquire a start of Buff Orphingtons, which were considered rare at that time. In hot weather, they would not roost in the chicken house, but preferred the nearest tree. An owl killed several nice, fat hens before Mama discovered the culprit. She waited patiently one night until Mr. Owl showed. She could hardly believe her eyes as she watched him gently nudge a hen to the end of the limb, then grab its throat as it fell. Mama shot the owl. She did not lose any chickens for a while.

There was a rock quarry not far from the cabin, and when the miners were paid, some of them would have a party in the old quarry. Mama would keep Opal and me inside when Dad went to work. We stayed inside with the doors locked while the parties were in progress.

One summer, an old hen stole her nest under the cabin and hatched every egg. The chicks were content to stay there. They became nice, fat fryers, roosting under the edge of the cabin.

Our dog, Bess, was an excellent dog, but she had one fault. She had been trained to let Dad come in when he came from work at night. The trouble was, she let only one man come inside the yard. That was fine if it were Dad, but if a neighbor or Uncle David happened to come by after Dad had gone to work, she would not let Dad come in until Mama gave her command. Dad always said Mama could not keep it a secret if a gentleman came calling!

One night, we were sleeping when the fryers were disturbed. Mama got her pistol and went to see what the trouble might be. Much to her surprise, a man was running up the alley with his hands full of chickens. She yelled for him to halt and drop the chickens, but he kept running. She gave chase and opened fire. She shot again, but the thief got away. She was so angry that her eyes snapped like fire. She sat up until Dad came from work.

Dad seldom said anything harsh to Mama, but this time he scolded her. "Ida, what in the world did you mean, running after that thief?

Don't you know he could have turned on you and taken the gun from you and killed you, or worse?" He pleaded, "Please promise me you won't do such a foolish thing again."

The next day, Dad bought Mama a shotgun. She practiced until she was a crack shot. She killed hawks that were after her chickens, rabbits and squirrels for dinner, and birds for blackbird pie. No snake got away if she saw him first.

But the fat hens began to disappear again. This time there were no telltale signs, as when the owl had killed them, for they were roosting inside the henhouse. They always came up missing on pay night at the mines.

Mama suggested that we go for a walk. She led us near the rock quarry. There were feathers, and that made her certain that she was furnishing chicken to go with the keg of beer.

The next payday rolled around, and the usual crowd gathered. Before dark, Mama took her shotgun, strolled over to the group and said, "If any more of my chickens disappear, I'm going to shoot up your playhouse, and you in it!"

The men told her they were sorry they had stolen her hens, and they offered to pay for them. But she told them emphatically that the only pay she wanted was for them to leave the chickens on the roost where they belonged. She did not intend to furnish drunks with a banquet!

All went smoothly until another brood of chicks grew into fryers.

Again, that silly dog let one man into the yard, and he grabbed the fryers. Mama went after him with her shotgun. "Halt!" *Blam!* "Drop those chickens!" *Blam! Blam!* He got away, but she was never bothered with thieves after that, as long as we lived in that cabin.

Our family doctor was a good friend. Soon after this shooting, he saw Mama and said, "Dag nab it, Ida, you kept me up all night, picking shot out of a fellow. By the way, he had a scar from a pistol shot that grazed his ribs on the left side. If you had used buckshot instead of bird shot, you would have killed him, and if that pistol shot had veered a little …"

"Yes, Doctor, but I was not trying to kill him. I just wanted him to drop my chickens."

The doctor laughed, and he would never tell the identity of the thief. ❖

—Originally published in August 1979.

That Darned Clock

By Ruth Owens

*T*ick-tock. Tick-tock. The steady, ponderous sound fills our house as the old kitchen mantel clock ticks away the hours. It is a family possession that we regard with pride and affection, an inseparable part of our daily lives, and the sound of its ticking is heartwarming and comforting. Yet, that old clock has not always been thought of in such endearing terms.

The old clock came into our family in 1905. Maudie Jane, my grandmother, was 13 then, and very ill. The doctor was sent for, and after examining her and diagnosing her illness, he left a bottle of medicine with her mother, gravely stating that a dose must be administered every hour.

After the doctor had gone, there was great consternation in the family. Mommie and Poppie, as Grandmother called her parents, discussed the matter. They had no clock—had never had one—and there was nothing to do but buy one.

Poppie hitched up the buggy and drove to the nearest town, a trip that took nearly all day. He returned late in the evening with the kitchen mantel clock. It was their first clock, and they were proud of it. It had leaves and scrolls carved on the frame, and scrolls were painted in gold on the small glass door, behind which the heavy, ornate pendulum could be seen. It had bold, black Roman numerals that were easy to read and a key for winding it.

> *"Thieves! Thieves!" she shrieked.*
> *"They're breaking down the door!"*

In every conceivable way, it seemed the ideal clock. But that changed at bedtime. In the bustle of getting the other children to bed and settling Maudie Jane comfortably for the night, no one noticed the clock's loud ticking. But after the lamp was blown out, and Mommie and Poppie were in bed and the house was quiet, the clock made itself heard.

Tick-tock! Tick-tock! Tick-tock! The sound thundered through the house and echoed back. Parents and children alike tossed and turned restlessly, seeking sleep that was denied by that slow, solemn ticking.

At last, exhaustion and worry took its toll, and the family went to sleep. Their rest, however, was abruptly and rudely shattered by a loud *Wham! Wham! Wham! Wham!*

Mommie screamed, flinging back the bedcovers back. "Thieves! Thieves!" she shrieked. "They're breaking down the door!" Poppie leaped from the bed, his bare feet thudding on the floor as he plunged across the room and jerked down the gun from its rack over the door.

Wham! Wham! Wham! Wham!

He halted in disgust, and with a shamefaced grin, turned back to Mommie.

"It's that darned clock! I'll give Maudie Jane her medicine." That was the debut of that old kitchen clock in our family.

As days passed, Maudie Jane improved. By the time she was well enough to sit up, the family had almost grown accustomed to the clock's ponderous ticking and thunderous striking.

One evening, Mommie and Poppie wrapped Maudie Jane in a quilt and set her by the fireplace, cautioning her to stay there until they had finished their chores. Now, Maudie Jane was a very determined person, and she wanted some popcorn. It was fall, and the popcorn was in the garden, ready to harvest, but it hadn't been gathered. After sitting there for a while, listening to the slow, solemn ticking that seemed to say "You can! You can!" Maudie Jane made up her mind that she would have some popcorn.

She threw off the quilt and started for the garden. She was very weak, but she was very determined. Halfway around the house, however, she discovered that her illness had left her weaker than she realized. She didn't make it to the garden.

Her recovery suffered a setback as a result, and once again she was confined to bed with the sound of the old clock's ticking for company.

As she and her sisters grew to womanhood, the ticking of the old clock kept pace as they sewed, quilted and worked around the house. In later years, Maudie Jane laughed about spying on her sisters and their beaus. Catching the entire family out one day, she crawled into the closet under the stairs and bored a hole through the wall into the parlor. She examined the hole on the parlor wall side to be sure it wouldn't be noticed. Then, when her sisters' beaus came calling, she would sneak into the closet and listen. Any rustling noises she might have made were covered by the ticking of the old clock. Later, she would mystify her sisters by repeating some of the things they and their beaus had said.

By now, the clock had become a valued and beloved family possession.

The years passed and "that darned clock," as my great-grandfather had once called it, ticked on until his death in 1946. Then my great-grandmother sadly stopped it, and the old clock sat there in majestic silence while complete quiet reigned throughout the old home.

In 1954, my great-grandmother died, and in dividing up the family possessions, the clock passed to Maudie Jane, my grandmother. After three sleepless nights and days spent echoing my great-grandfather's "that darned clock" complaint, she gave it to my mother.

My mother was not enthusiastic. She and that old clock had been archenemies during her childhood, when she visited her grandparents and spent the night with them. However, that had been years ago, and perhaps it wasn't as terrible as she remembered. But it was. Our sleep was rudely disrupted. But the clock stayed, and we rapidly adjusted to the noise. Now, instead of calling it "that darned clock," we referred to it most proudly as "our clock."

It did affect our lives in some odd ways. First, it cut down on the time we spent cooking and washing. We had out-of-state relatives who often visited, staying with us for a night or two. But with the arrival of the old clock, that changed. After one night of tossing and turning, listening to "that darned clock" ticking away and whamming out the hour, they changed their habits. They would visit us during the day, but at night they would stay with other relatives in the area.

As the years passed, we made the surprising discovery that the old clock had become so much a part of our lives that we had to stop and listen to its ponderous ticking. The thunderous striking of the hour no longer alarms us; much more frightening is that deep, brooding, oppressive silence that fills the house on the rare occasions when the winding of the old clock has been forgotten.

Tick-tock! Tick-tock! The old clock sits on its shelf in the kitchen, the heavy, ornate pendulum still steadily swinging back and forth as it ticks away the minutes, still accurately keeping time. Its original title of "that darned clock" has been all but forgotten, and is revived only when the family reminisces. As I listen to it wham out the hour, I'm thankful my great-grandfather bought "that darned clock." ❖

—Originally published in August 1979.

SEPT., 1981

75¢

47312

GOOD·OLD·DAYS

Featuring:

LETTERS * STORIES

* PHOTOS * POEMS * CARTOONS * SONGS * ILLUSTRATIONS *of the Happy Days Gone By*

THE MAGAZINE OF HAPPY MEMORIES

0 72246 47073 2

The '80s:
A New Home

Chapter Three

Getting to know a new home is never easy, especially when you have lived in the same place for a long time. I was born and raised in the same house, living there until my wife and I married. It was then that I discovered just how tough it is to move to new environs, no matter how nice your new home might be.

That really wasn't the way it was when *Good Old Days* found itself in a new home in 1985. Ed Kutlowski, who with his brother Mike founded House of White Birches, retired from the publishing business and sold the company to another pair of brothers, Art and Carl Muselman, of Berne, Ind.

Good Old Days could not have been transplanted in better soil.

The brothers were second generation publishers and printers born to Christian and Edna Muselman, hard-working parents of Swiss descent. The Muselman brothers, both deceased now, were two of the finest people I have ever had the privilege to meet. Their strong ties to God, their family and their country were perfectly aligned with the readership of *Good Old Days*.

Berne is a village northeast of Indianapolis, named after the capital of Switzerland, its citizens proud of their heritage. It is also in the heart of Indiana Amish country, appropriate when you think of the simple, old-fashioned ways remembered in the pages of the magazine.

Good Old Days went through a rapid succession of three editors in four years after moving to its new home.

Then, as the decade of the '80s was coming to a close, John Robinson—the chief executive officer of House of White Birches—tracked down Janice and me. John and I had been colleagues in Texas before he moved to Indiana, and he knew my wife and I had moved back to her old home place in Arkansas. It was our intent to let our last years roll by watching the grass grow and other such exhilerating fare.

But John would have none of it.

He convinced me to come out of editorial retirement and help him with *Good Old Days*. Now, nearly two decades later, we're still in the saddle and looking toward the magazine's golden anniversary.

In its own way, *Good Old Days* became our new home. We have gained so many new family members in all of those years. We have read tens of thousands of letters, stories and poems written by our dear readers. They have come to us handwritten on lacey stationery, typed on old Royal uprights and, yes, even laser-printed from laptops. And we have been humbled by our readers' willingness to let us tell their stories.

A new home usually signals a new start, whether you are talking about a marriage or a magazine. *Good Old Days* found a new home and renewed vitality as these stories from the 1980s demonstrate.

—Ken Tate

The Day I Met Dick Tracy

By R. Elizabeth Burke

When I see my nephews and niece enjoying *The Hardy Boys* and *Nancy Drew* on TV and proudly hanging up the latest giant poster of their TV heroes, I find myself remembering the time when radio serials were so very popular with the same age group. However, the faces of those heroes were never seen—no magazine pinups, no posters, no newspaper interviews. In fact, we hardly knew their real names. The character was important, not the actor playing him. How strange it seems now that just voices could so hold us!

But I'll never forget the day I saw and met Dick Tracy. I was 7 or 8 years old. World War II was in full swing, and my father was overseas. I was old enough to miss him terribly and worry about him a lot. Perhaps as much for escape as for entertainment, I was totally "hooked" on the late-afternoon radio serials. *Hop Harrigan—America's Ace of the Airways*, *Superman*, *Terry and the Pirates*, *Jack Armstrong, the All-American Boy*, and my favorite, *Dick Tracy*. I loved them all.

I was totally "hooked" on the late-afternoon radio serials.

Every afternoon at 4:45, my mother, following my instructions, would call me in from play for my programs. Kids weren't given watches so young then, and I had to rely on Mom. She knew how much I looked forward to those daily episodes, and she never forgot to call me. I know, though, that she and my friends wondered how I could stop dead, day after day, in the middle of whatever we were doing to run home so I wouldn't miss a single minute.

I'd sit next to our radio, literally in another world. I was entranced as crisis after crisis was met and conquered by my heroes. Today, I enjoy many things on TV, but no form of entertainment ever stirred me like radio did in those days. What a marvelous world we created in our imaginations!

In early January 1944, Dad came home on leave. My baby sister had never met Daddy, and my next youngest sister didn't remember him, so we spent some days just getting reacquainted. Happy as I was to have him home, even for just a few weeks, I was positively ecstatic when he announced that just the two of us were going to New York City for the day. Although we lived on Long Island, trips to the city were not common for kids, especially in wartime.

Early the next morning, we boarded the train, and in a little over an hour, we were in Grand Central Station. We had a glorious day: going to the top of the Empire State Building, eating at an automat and just talking. But he saved the best treat for last.

Late in the afternoon, we entered what looked to me like a large office building. Then Dad said we were there to watch the *Dick Tracy* program. I couldn't believe it! All my friends and I knew that some radio shows had audiences, but we also knew that the 15-minute serials definitely did not. But Dad knew someone at the radio station (WOR), and that—plus his captain's uniform, I'm sure—was all the "in" we needed.

The program aired in a small studio while we watched from the control booth through a huge window. There really was no place for an audience to sit. I was amazed that the actors wore ordinary business suits, and all of them used only one microphone. After each one spoke his lines, he'd step aside for the next person.

It was a particularly exciting episode that day, with Dick Tracy menaced by the "Owl," a Nazi spy hiding out on a Western dude ranch. I was entranced the whole time. The sound effects, the signals to the actors from the booth, the red light that flashed on and off, even the Tootsie Roll commercials—I'd never seen anything like it or imagined that was the way it was done. I was fascinated.

When the broadcast was over, we were introduced to the cast, and they gave me a copy of the script, which I still have. It was a working copy, complete with crossed-out phrases and penciled-in cues.

Dad went back to war. I still missed him and worried about him, but my *Dick Tracy* script was the envy of all my friends. The glow from that day stayed with me for a long time.

A year and a half later, when we moved to California to join Dad who was now stationed there, I was amazed to discover that all my programs were heard three hours earlier in the West, while I was still in school. However, with our family now complete again, I didn't miss my programs as much as I thought I would. By the time we'd moved back East a year or so later, I'd outgrown them. They were fast disappearing by then, too.

Still, every once in a while, when people recall with nostalgia the old radio shows that are no more, I'll stop them cold by asking, "By the way, did I ever tell you about the time I met Dick Tracy?" ❖

—*Originally published in January 1980.*

The GI Haircut

By Lelias E. Kirby

My brother Amos is two years my senior. He always has felt that this seniority gives him the authority to advise me about everything I do. I have become so accustomed to it that I call him before making any decisions.

When World War I broke out, he talked me into enlisting in the Army with him. After a few days, Amos was transferred to headquarters company. He immediately began scheming to get me transferred, too.

When my company captain announced that there was a vacancy in the barbershop, and if anyone wished to be transferred to headquarters company, he should step three paces forward. I had never been in a barbershop, but I felt sure that Amos was behind this move. When I cast an inquiring eye at him, he nodded "yes."

I was the first to be interviewed. "Your name and rank?" I knew I was on a hot spot because the other two fellows who had stepped out were barbers by trade.

I answered, "Private Lelias E. Kirby, sir."

The officer then asked if I was related to Amos Kirby, who recently had transferred to headquarters company. This put me on still a hotter spot. If I said no, I was liable to be punished for lying as well as for being his brother. I knew that a soldier should be brave, so I admitted that we were brothers, and humbly apologized. Before I could finish, the officer interrupted me and told me to report to the barber tent and fix up as many boys as possible before inspection, which was to be in two hours.

Evidently the last customer had gotten a

shave, as the chair was lying back. I was unable to raise it. My first customer, however—my top sergeant—put the chair in its proper position.

On my first upward stroke, my clippers hung up. My efforts to disengage them started the most violent outburst of profanity that had ever tapped my eardrums. I stood in the corner of the tent while he gave his description of the kind of barber he thought I was. All the time I was trying to figure some way to release the clippers from his hair.

The idea came to me to cut them free with my scissors, and I did. With each succeeding stroke of the clippers, however, the same thing occurred, until I had peeled his head as slick as an onion. It was now time for inspection. The sergeant found that his hat was about two sizes too large, and there was no time to locate another hat before inspection.

All the high brass came down the line. Suddenly they all stopped to see what was under that hat. One of them removed it, and as he did, the highest ranker yelled, "Who cut your hair?"

"The official company barber, sir," the sergeant answered.

After a conference, the commanding officer blurted out, "That is the way I want them *all* cut!" This history-making episode took place on a Thursday, and on the following Saturday, General Pershing posted a general order on every bulletin board throughout the AEF ordering every soldier to have his hair cut to one quarter inch in length.

I have never been given due credit, but I'm the bird who originated the GI haircut. ❖

—Originally published in February 1980.

The Heater Came Down

By Rae Cross

I remember the humid day Father said, "I think it's warm enough. We can take down the heater." No sooner were the words said than Mother and I ran for the stack of newspapers we had been saving for the occasion. We covered everything in the room.

A kitchen chair was set in front of the flue into which the stovepipe fitted. Father got an empty coal bucket and the soot scraper, and then climbed onto the chair.

Carefully he removed the first joint of the long stovepipe. He handed it to Mother, who ran to the back yard with it and shook the soot into the ash pit. Joint after joint came down. Mother and I took turns running them to the back yard, trying hard not to spill any soot along the way.

When the final joint was down, Father took the scraper and pulled soot from the black tunnel into the coal bucket again and again until no more soot came out. Then he took the bucket of soot to the ash pit as well.

When he returned, he climbed back onto the chair and placed the flue cover over the yawning hole. How pretty it looked, with the purple pansies on it—and how big the room looked after the heater had been lugged out to the shed, where it would spend the summer.

Then it was Mother's turn. "Roll up the carpet. Take it out and hang it on the clothesline. Then get the rug beater and start using it."

That big old beater was heavy and awkward. Beating the rug with it was difficult, but it did make the dirt and dust give up their hold. It always seemed to me that the more I choked and coughed from the dust, the happier Mother was.

Curtains had to come down to be washed and pinned to the curtain stretchers. All around the four sides, the wet curtains had to be pinned to the stretchers and left to dry—preferably in the sun.

Walls and woodwork had to be washed. Windows were washed with vinegar and rubbed with paper until they sparkled. The floor was mopped. The furniture was polished. Papers were laid on the floor three deep before the beaten rug was brought back in.

When the curtains were dry, all the pins had to be removed and the rods run through the curtains. The curtains were hung in place, starched stiff and Fels-Naphtha clean. Then the furniture was returned to its accustomed place; the pictures were hung; and the taboret, with its marble top, was placed close to the door, with a silver salver resting on its polished surface, waiting to hold visitors' calling cards. How proud Mother was of those cards, each representing a friend.

Father and I dropped onto the porch swing. Mother stood in the middle of the clean room, smoothing her apron as she sized up the day's work. No words were uttered, but how plainly her expression said, "This is my home, and it is good. Let the Ladies' Aid or whomever come—they can find nothing to criticize."

Mentally, Father and I agreed. Another spring and summer had come; the heater was down, the room was clean. "We had better go polish the heater," sighed Father, "and clean and polish those stove joints. Before we know it, it will be time to put it back up again." ❖

—Originally published in May 1980.

The Most Beautiful Dress in the World

By Elba Vassar

When I was almost 4 years old, my mother had the most beautiful dress in the world. Whenever we went somewhere important, like family reunions, weddings or the Christmas church program, Mother was the prettiest lady there. She had sparkling eyes, a peachy smooth complexion and gorgeous auburn hair, and she always wore that dress.

She told me it was her wedding dress, and she saved it to wear to special places. It was silk with lace—not white, not yellow, but just about the color of old Bossie's cream. Oh, how I loved to feel the soft fabric! I told Mother that when I grew up, I'd have one exactly like it.

Mother would smile and push my stubborn brown hair out of my eyes and say, "I'm sure you'll have one much prettier some day."

It was a dress, soft and sliky, like I'd always dreamed of.

She was a seamstress, and any piece of material she sewed turned out to be a pretty dress for me. I liked my dresses with flowers and checks and stripes, but no matter what dress I wore, I dreamed of that delicate silk and lace dress Mother said I'd have some day. A dress like that was worth waiting for.

My father had a job at the feed store in 1933, but one day he was hurt. As long as I live, I'll remember the dark look on my mother's face when the doctor told her my father's back was broken.

Daddy was in bed for a long time, but Mother kept smiling. She worked all the time and didn't play games with me anymore. All day long she made hominy and sometimes baked cakes and pies for people who had enough money to pay for them.

Daddy kept telling Mother he worried about her working so hard while he was sick, but she always said she didn't mind and told him not to worry so much.

Then he got well and went back to his job. But before long, he came home again and sat down at the kitchen table. I thought I saw a tear in his eye when he finally said, "They gave my job to John the day I got hurt. I don't have a job any more. What will we do?"

Mother looked sad for a few minutes, but then she said, "It won't be forever. You'll get another job, and we can make it somehow." Then she got up and made more hominy. I'll never forget the flat, salty smell of hominy in the kitchen. I couldn't imagine anyone wanting that much hominy day after day.

After that, I liked Daddy better even though he wasn't working a job because he took me hunting or fishing with him almost every day. We at least had rabbit, squirrel, or fish for supper. Even fish frying smelled better than hominy or the black-eyed peas Mother cooked.

Every Sunday when we went to church, Mother and Daddy and I were always spanking clean. Our shoes sparkled even though the soles were getting thin. Mother said it was important to look neat and clean, but I remember the color in my dresses wasn't as bright as it used to be, and neither were my mother's eyes. Daddy didn't look as happy as he used to, either, but I thought we were having more fun than we had before.

Later, Mother and Daddy didn't go to church every Sunday, but Grandma and Uncle Daily took me. Mother and Daddy didn't go, they said, because there wasn't enough money to put in the collection plate. But I always had a penny, and I never had to miss Sunday school.

I remember especially when the next Sunday was going to be my birthday and Grandma promised me a surprise to wear to Sunday school. I woke up early that day, and sure enough, Grandma was there with my present. It was a new pair of red patent-leather Roman sandals. I'd never seen prettier shoes, but even they didn't compare to the present Mother gave me. It was a dress, soft and silky, like I'd always dreamed of. It had lace, too, all across the yoke, all the way up to my neck, and on the bottom of my skirt and sleeves—and not only that, but it was as near the color of Mother's beautiful dress as I could ever hope for.

I put it on, and when I looked in the mirror, it was every bit as pretty as Mother's dress. That day, everyone at church told me how pretty my new birthday clothes were. I was as proud as I could be.

Later that week, my mother's best friend came to visit us. She was excited about their class reunion the next week. Then I heard Mother say that she couldn't go because she didn't have a decent dress to wear.

"Of course you do. Wear your ecru silk. That dress is just perfect," her friend said.

"I don't have it anymore," Mother told her softly.

Suddenly, it hit me. I ran from the room to the closet in Mother's bedroom. Her dress wasn't there. I crept to her sewing basket. There, just as I expected, I found a few pieces of cream-colored silk folded neatly, some lace wound on a card, and several round pearl buttons strung on a safety pin.

I pulled my dress from the hanger and held it tightly, for at that moment, I knew that I really did have the dress I'd always wanted. I sat on my bed for a long time, and just before I finally fell asleep, my tears made dark spots on my dress. I cried because at that age, I couldn't understand why I felt the way I did about the most beautiful dress in the world that had been made and given to me by the greatest lady on earth. ❖

—Originally published
in November 1984.

Hide in the Dark

By Ada Breise Cromer

*M*y friend, Sally, lived with her 80-year-old Grandmother Kinsley. She was an alert, friendly, good-natured grandma who let us have the run of the house. All of us who knew her called her "Granny." She liked to have young people around her. This was the reason we chose Sally's home for our Saturday-night parties in the 1920s.

Granny took an interest in everything we did. There were six of us girls, including Sally. Sometimes we sat around the fireplace, eating popcorn and roasting marshmallows and listening to Granny tell thrilling stores of her youth. She enjoyed an attentive audience. She loved a good story, and she was adept at keeping us in suspense.

Usually we spent an entire night at Grandma Kinsley's house, and it was just as well that we did, because some of her haunting, ghostly tales left us scared of our own shadows.

I looked forward to those Saturday nights during my teenage years. Sometimes we made candy or played bingo, or we played our favorite records on Granny's old wind-up phonograph and danced to the music.

Our favorite pastime was an exciting game we called Hide in the Dark. It had materialized from our lively imaginations after a book I had read. Grandma Kinsley's house was ideal for playing Hide in the Dark because it was a large, rambling domicile of many rooms. It was built in Colonial style, a three-story affair, including the attic, which was used for storage.

Usually Sally was allowed to hide first because it was her home. But one Saturday night, her city cousin, Barbara, was spending the weekend there, and it was her birthday. Barbara was given the privilege of choosing a hiding place anywhere in the house except Granny's living room. Since Barbara visited Sally occasionally, she was familiar with the rooms, closets, the basement and attic.

The game was fairly simple. A record was played on the phonograph from beginning to end, which took three or four minutes. With the lights turned out, we sat with our heads face-down on our arms. The music drowned

out all sounds during the hider's getaway. The moment the music stopped, we dashed to our feet and began our search. The first to find the hiding place could hide next.

On this night, when the last note of the record had sounded, we scattered throughout the house, searching and groping along hallways and up and down stairways. There was a full moon that night, and it helped to guide us. We shrieked and laughed as we bumped into one another. Sometimes a hand came out of the dark and grabbed an arm.

We searched for almost an hour, but no Barbara. "Where can she be?" someone yelled.

"We've looked everywhere," Sally called, "except in the attic. But that's so full of junk, she couldn't squeeze past the door."

Granny had been dozing by the fire in her rocking chair with her hands folded in her lap. The firelight touched her face and the gray of her hair made weird shadows on the walls and ceiling. At the word *attic* she came suddenly wide awake. "The attic!" she yelled. She turned up the lamp beside her chair, sat up straight, and stared at us as we gathered around her.

"There's an old trunk up there," she told us.

"But Granny," Sally said, "it's chockful of old clothes."

"It *was*," Granny corrected. "Moths got in them, and I gave them all to the ragman."

"Let's look anyway," I said. "She's got to be in the attic."

And that is where we found Barbara, curled up like a kitten, and plenty mad and disgusted because it had taken us so long. When we got her downstairs, all the lights were on and Granny had a strange story to tell us.

"When I was a girl," she told us, "there was a wedding, and the young folks played a game much like this one you play. The bride was the one who hid, and everyone went scurrying around trying to find her. Then they lit all the lamps and went about with flashlights, yelling and threatening her with scary things like scalding her in hot water or pulling all her hair out if she didn't come out. It was no use. After midnight, they all gave up and went home.

"The groom was fit to be tied. The only thing they could figure out was that she had had a change of heart and ran away with an old beau who had shown up at the wedding. Since he'd left town, there was that much more reason to believe that it had all been arranged."

Granny got up and silently poked at the dying fire. She looked at us sitting quietly on the floor. She reseated herself in her rocker and slowly rocked to and fro. Then she continued.

"She was a pretty little thing, with long, blond curls and eyes as blue as cornflowers."

"Did they ever find out what became of her?" I asked.

"Oh, yes," Granny said, "I was coming to that. She'd never left the place."

"Several years later, she was found in an old sea chest in the attic."

Six pairs of eyes studied Granny's face. This was the suspenseful moment she liked best. "What? How come? Why?" we questioned, waiting for the clincher.

"Several years later, she was found in an old sea chest in the attic," Granny explained. "Just a skeleton in what had been her long, white dress, and her skull framed in what was left of her wedding veil. The heavy lid of the old chest had locked and she suffocated."

For about seven seconds there was utter silence. Granny's eyes twinkled mischievously as she looked at our sober faces.

"Oh, how horrible," Sally said, and most of us echoed her thoughts. "How awful!"

I turned to look at Barbara. "Oh, well," she said, "my old trunk didn't have a heavy lid, and it didn't lock."

Sally was gazing thoughtfully into space. She liked to hang onto a story as long as she could. As usual, she had a question. "What became of the groom, Grann?"

Granny, half-asleep, awoke with a start.

"Groom? Oh, him. He married someone else. Fickle he was. She was well rid of him."

Sally and Barbara sat cozily by the fireplace. Granny was again nodding in her chair. It was time for the rest of us to leave, clutching one another like four scaredy cats. It was the last time we played Hide in the Dark. ❖

—Originally published in January 1985.

GOOD·OLD·DAYS

$1.35
K47312

FEBRUARY
1985

Featuring:

LETTERS STORIES
PHOTOS • POEMS • CARTOONS • SONGS • ILLUSTRATIONS *of the Happy Days Gone By*

The Underdog

By Michelle Coffman

Elsie was the 10th of 11 children born to Earl and Hope Arnett. Born in Dexter, N.M., in 1932, she moved to Texas, then back to New Mexico, before finally settling near Turlock, Calif. She had been moving around all her life and hoped her family would stay put at Turlock for a while. They moved so much that she attended second grade at four schools in three states.

Elsie was in the seventh grade now, going to school in the Ballico School District. It was during the Second World War. The Japanese were sent to concentration camps, and their farms were available for yearly leasing. Earl leased one of these farms, raising livestock, fruit, nuts, grapes and persimmons. It was a nice place with a big house, and they were very happy there.

Timid as she was, with changing school so much, Elsie always made a friend. She had a nice friend her age named Nevee. Nevee had a not-so-nice brother in the eighth grade; he made two of little Nevee, who was small for her age. George was so mean that I think his main subject in school was making as many people as possible miserable.

One time, Elsie had injured herself on the back of her ankle. A scab had formed, and it was very painful. When Elsie got to school, whenever George got the chance, he would come up from behind and scrape her ankle with his boots, tearing at the scab!

Goodness knows what his little sister was subjected to at home, but at school, George tormented her mercilessly. One day, something must have been eating at George, for at recess, he came up to little Nevee, doubled his fist, and punched her so hard in the stomach that she bent over, falling to the ground in pain.

Elsie saw it happen. When she saw Nevee collapse, her fierce defense of the underdog took over! Elsie flew into George, knocking him down in the dirt, working him over until he had no doubts that he had been worked over! Elsie was wearing a big ring on her finger she had borrowed that day, and by the time she peeled herself off poor George, she found the ring broken and the stones scattered.

The teacher—a man—came quickly running out to the playground, and big tough George got up with a bloody nose, boo-hooing his head off.

Well, the teacher told Elsie to go home—that she was expelled from school. She had to walk quite a ways before getting home, but already the teacher was there in the yard before her, talking to her dad in choppy, angered tones.

Her dad called her over and asked, "Is this true what the teacher says? Did you hit a boy after he punched his sister?"

"Yes, I did, Daddy," answered Elsie.

At that point, the poor teacher, wanting and expecting fireworks, must have suffered a great disappointment, for Earl looked down at his daughter and patted her on the shoulder. "Well, good for you, sister!" he said, smiling. "Good for you!" Earl always defended the underdog, and he was pleased and proud that his daughter had done the same.

To be sure, George acquired a new respect for Elsie. He became the perfect little gentleman around her ever after, until his family moved away a few months later. The teacher was most kind now, too.

The Arnetts lived on that farm for about two years. Then the Japanese were released from the concentration camps and returned to their homes. The Japanese family praised Earl and his family for taking such good care of their farm. Then the Arnetts moved to another place in Turlock.

Elsie is my mother, and a grandmother now, and I'm proud to say that she has never changed. She is always ready to help and defend the underdog. ❖

—Originally published in February 1985.

Facing page: *Good Old Days* magazine cover, February 1985, House of White Birches nostalgia archives

Prisoners of War

By Frances Innes

*M*y husband and I and our four children and my father were prisoners of war in the Philippines during World War II. Years before the war, my husband had been sent to the Islands as a teacher, and Manila was home to our four children. My husband was taken prisoner as soon as the war began, but for the first year, the rest of us were allowed to stay in our home. That was because the Japanese loved children and respected old people. But as the war got worse, we were all put in prison.

We were sent first to the new campus of Santo Tomas University at the edge of Manila. This prison happened to be the oldest university under the American flag. It had been started by Catholic priests in 1611. The Japanese found it an ideal spot to put prisoners because there was a big fence around it, part stone and part iron bars.

Of course, the children missed their home. At the start, Jim was 10, Don was 12, Frank about 6, and Chuck was only a year old.

We looked toward the hills and saw men with guns rushing toward us.

After a year, the prison became so crowded that we were moved to the agricultural campus at Los Banos. We were less comfortable here, and food was getting scarce. We were always hungry. Food rations got smaller and smaller. To feed my children, I traded my engagement ring for a sack of rice.

At the Los Banos prison, we had tiny rooms with wooden floors, but the partitions and ceiling were swali grass. The bathrooms were in another building opposite our barracks.

On the morning of Jan. 23, 1945, I was over there taking a bath when Chuck, now 4, came screaming as though a tiger were after him. He was screaming so that I could not make out what he was trying to say. I shut off the water and listened at the door. I heard yells: "Mexicans! Mexicans!" We had heard rumors that Americans were coming, but there had been false rumors before, so I did not know what to believe. I threw on my ragged clothes as fast as I could and hurried out. Still panic-stricken, Chuck was clutching my skirt. He had no idea what "Mexicans" were.

Now I saw big parachutes coming down from the sky. They were Americans! Tears of happiness welled in my eyes. I cried, "It's all right, Chuck! They've come to set us free!" But Chuck had never seen a parachute, and he was crying and choking, frightened half to death.

Then the American soldiers came running, each with a gun under one arm and a handful of goodies for the children. They were playing Santa Claus, handing out chocolate bars to our starving children. As soon as Chuck got a piece of candy, his screaming stopped, and wonder and happiness replaced his tears.

But a few minutes later, panic struck again. We looked toward the hills and saw men with guns rushing toward us. They were too short to be Americans. Someone shouted, "Guerrillas!"

They came out of the trees toward us. At first I did not know whether they were on our side or the other side, and I was terrified. Of course, the children were terrified, too. We were all shaking.

Then the American soldiers said, "They are with us! The Filipino guerrillas are on our side!"

What a relief! The Japanese guards had been caught completely by surprise. A man named Peter Miles had escaped from our prison and gotten to an American officer with the word that our

guards stacked their guns each morning at 7 o'clock and lined up for calisthenics, so the morning attack had caught them unarmed.

Now we were told to go to the nearby lake. We hesitated. My father was trying to get his valise from beneath his cot. To get us away, soldiers set fire to the back of our prison barracks.

"Come! You'll get burned! Come right now!" I yelled at my father, tugging at him. We all ran to the lake.

We saw amtraks, huge amphibian tractors, crawling out of the lake like prehistoric monsters. When Chuck screamed again, I quieted him by telling him that the soldiers who had given him the candy had come on these tractors. We were hurried onto the tractors, packed as tight as could be, with standing room only. Then the amtraks took us out over barbed wire and across the lake to the headquarters that had been set up by the Americans as soon as they landed.

It was wonderful to feel safe and secure again, among our own people.

We were all skin and bones, too starved and shaky to be shipped home right away. The Japanese were short on food for themselves, so, of course, we did not get much.

The U.S. Army officer in charge put us in a comfortable house at the edge of Manila and gave us lots of wholesome American food. You should have seen my children eat! They really enjoyed that food. Little Chuck had never seen bread and potatoes and milk. He said, "Gosh, Mom, this is good! What do you call it?"

After we had added some pounds and gained strength, we were put aboard ship and sent to the West Coast of the United States and then on to join our relatives. ❖

—Originally published in November 1985.

Where Babies Come From

By James Harold Price

We knew a baby was coming. The rocking cradle had been brought down from the attic, made up with clean white sheets and a new quilt, and placed by Mama's side of the bed. The family did a lot of whispering that we younger ones weren't supposed to hear, but we had an idea what they were talking about.

Sis stayed home from school, which she never did unless she was sick in bed. She was up early, acting like a mama, bossing us around.

"Go outside and play in the front yard, both of you, and don't come in until I call you. Don't go in the road. A car might come by."

We sat on the front steps awhile, wondering why we had to stay outside. I asked my brother, "Charles, do you know where babies come from?"

"The stork brings 'em."

"What's a stork?"

"A big bird with a long nose."

"Have you ever seen one?"

"I saw a picture of one carrying a baby hanging in a diaper."

I was dubious. "I've never seen a bird big enough to carry a baby!"

"Then where do you think babies come from?" he demanded.

"The doctor brings 'em."

"Who told you that?"

"Lucy."

"Lucy's a girl. Girls don't know anything."

"Yes she does! She saw the doctor bring her little brother!"

"Well, Papa told me the stork brought you."

Papas are supposed to know everything, so I couldn't argue anymore. Still, Lucy was my best friend and never told me anything that wasn't true.

We heard a car coming from far down the road. In those days, hearing a car was exciting. Seeing one was really special. I guessed at once it must be the doctor bringing the baby, but then I wasn't sure who was right, Lucy or Charles. Charles didn't always tell the truth and Lucy did.

The doctor's Model A stopped right in front of our house. He got out, put a rock under the front wheel, then took a little bag from the front seat. As he walked across the front yard toward the house, my eyes were glued to that little black bag. It wasn't much larger than Sis' pencil box!

I whispered, "Charles, the baby must be in that bag!"

"Naw. That isn't big enough for a baby."

"Yes, it is too! Wait and see."

Sis came to the door and opened it for the doctor. "You boys stay in the yard until I call you," she told us. Then she went inside after the doctor.

Charles was sure the stork was coming. "Snooks, run around to the backyard and watch for the stork to come. I'll watch the front. Call me if you see it."

I sat on the back steps, watching the sky just in case Charles was right.

I wasn't too sure a baby would fit into that little bag. I thought a lot about it while I waited for the stork to fly by.

Maybe babies were like balloons and could be blown up—maybe babies were so soft they could be squeezed into a little bag.

It seemed a long time before I heard the doctor cranking his car. I ran around to the front to watch. After many spins of the handle and adjustments of the spark and gas, the motor sputtered and started. The doctor waved to us as he drove down the road, leaving behind a cloud of dust much bigger than any wagon or buggy ever made.

Soon Sis appeared on the front porch. "You can come on in now," she said. "You can meet your new baby sister."

As we approached the house, I asked Charles, "Did you see the stork?"

"Naw. Did you?"

"All I saw was a robin with a worm, but he didn't come to the house. He flew on up to the apple tree."

Charles and I approached Mama's room slowly. We weren't sure what to expect.

"Come in and see your new sister," Mama called. "She's beautiful."

The baby was wrapped in a blanket and tucked in the cradle. We could only see the tiny face, beet red and wrinkled like a prune. Speechless, we stared at her, wondering if she would grow up to be a person.

My concern finally got the best of me, and I broke the silence: "Mama? Don't you think the doctor should get a larger bag?" ❖

—Originally published in January 1986.

GOOD·OLD·DAYS

FEATURING:
LETTERS - STORIES - PHOTOS - CARTOONS - SONGS - ILLUSTRATIONS

JULY 1986 $1.35 $1.60 CANADA

GARDEN
V FOR VICTORY

K47312

John Slobodnik

Love Me, Love My Horse

By Carl Wolfgang Maiwald

My pa's favorite story was about the time his sister Kate got the whole village of Larkin Corners in an uproar over the caper she pulled right in front of the Hard-Shell Baptist Church. Her bold dash for freedom kept the gossips in ammunition for weeks as their tales grew wilder with each telling. Some of the worst tattlers claimed my aunt rode over her lover and trampled him to death, but that was really stretching things!

Pa was one of the last of the old storytellers. He'd learned the art from his Grandma Eckmann. The old lady had nary a bit of "book larnin'," but she had the whole family's history crammed in her head, along with dozens of the most wonderful tales to fit any occasion. She was at her best when she was rocking gently by the fireplace and puffing on her clay pipe. As the flickering shadows leaped and danced on walls and ceilings, she'd hold her listeners spellbound with her stories of elves, witches and just plain folks in amusing situations. And the wide-eyed little tyke who loved to listen to his granny's tales later became my father.

Aunt Kate scandalized the prim folks of Larkin Corners.

My pa, like his tutor, was at his best on a long winter evening when all the chores were done and the family was gathered in our parlor. He'd blow out the coal oil lamp and light one candle that turned the organ and the Edison phonograph into shapeless, brooding hulks that his vivid words could turn into anything from a settler's sod shanty to a circus elephant. Stuffing his old briar with Prince Albert, he'd puff away while we decided which story we wanted to hear. Then he'd keep us enraptured until bedtime.

This is how I recall his story of Aunt Kate and how she scandalized the prim folks of Larkin Corners.

Kate was the oldest of us three kids. She was a year older than Nettie and five years older than me. She never cared much for housework, and she was always ready to help Pa and me with the farm chores, which was all right with Nettie, who liked being Ma's helper.

Like most of the hill country farms, ours had a couple of hundred acres of rough, brushy land that were good only for pasture. Sometimes when Pa opened the barn door and yodeled "Co-boos, co-baw-aws!"

in the time-honored cattle call, the cows would come trooping in to take their places in the milking barn; then again, they might stay put out in the hills. That's when Sis would throw a saddle and bridle on Snicker, her strawberry roan gelding, and roust the lazy critters out of their hiding places in the brush. Kate was the one who ran the errands, like taking soup to a sick neighbor or going after the doctor or veterinarian (we had no telephone, of course), because she and Snicker could make the trip in half the time it would take in our buckboard.

If the situation was bad, like when Nettie got the 'pendicitis attack, Kate and that loyal horse would travel like the wind to bring help. She was a regular angel of mercy on horseback to shut-ins and sick folks. She was something else to some lonely fellers. Half the bachelors in Danford County had an eye on her as good wife material, but she never paid much heed to their coaxing, nor would she dance two square sets with the same partner. It seemed like she would be Pa's hired hand forever.

Then the love bug bit her. And the amazing thing was that it wasn't a local man who swept her off her feet, but a real city dude with fancy clothes and a smooth line of sweet talk! I had been hoping she would marry Jake Purdy, the bachelor who had a farm down the road a piece, but Kate wasn't the kind to take advice from a kid brother she'd helped raise, so I knew enough to keep my opinion of the city slicker to myself.

I happened to be with her when she met Throcky. It was like this:

We were at the shooting gallery at the Danford County Fair, Sis and me only, as the rest of the family had gone onto the giant Ferris wheel that lofted folks high over the treetops. I had just run up a score of 19 moving targets out of 25 knocked off, and Kate was trying to beat my count. She tipped over the moving iron ducks with monotonous regularity, then picked up another rifle to show she could do it again.

Photo courtesy of House of White Birches nostalgia archives

"That red-haired beauty is a veritable Annie Oakley," said a slick voice in my ear—and there he was, a dude in fancy suit and gray derby.

Kate turned to see who it was, so the slicker bowed deeply as he swept his derby in a wide swing. "May I introduce myself?" he gurgled. "I'm Harrison—"

"Hmph!" interrupted Kate, turning back to her shooting. But her skill had deserted her; she missed five targets in a row. "Come on, Bub," she snapped. "Let's get something to eat."

We moseyed over to the tent where the ladies of our church had set up a long table heaped with fried chicken, smashed potatoes, roasting ears and all the trimmings. You helped yourself to all you could cram down for a quarter. A glass of milk and a hunk of cherry, peach or apple pie was 10 cents more; seconds on the pie were free. I ate until my belly hurt, then ate some more.

Looking up from my plate, I noticed the dude sitting just across the table. He was picking at his food and eyeing Kate, who was doing likewise. Seeing I was stuffed to the gills, my sister suggested we go watch the hog-calling contest.

As we left the feast, I snuck a look at the city slicker. He dropped a five spot on the table and waved off the change. He stuck with us through the hog calling, the quilt judging and the horse-pulling contest. I kept wondering when our shadow would call it quits.

Then we ran into our minister, Rev. Baird. The reverend, who happened to know the dude dogging our footsteps, introduced him as "Harrison Pendergast Throckmorton, the third."

Sis gave him her bone-crusher handshake and a polite "Pleezeta-meetcha."

He almost yelped in pain, then put Sis' calloused hand to his lips as he purred, "Call me Throcky. I'm smitten by your grace and beauty."

What a ham; Sis will see right through him, I figured. But I figured wrong. She kind of simpered and let him take us on the rides at the fair.

He said that he just happened to be in Larkin Corners on business, but was an apprentice in his father's undertaking parlor in Port Chester. *Good. Living 50 miles away should keep the guy from making a nuisance of himself,* I decided.

Wrong again. Every dang weekend, he'd take the train to Larkin Corners, hire a buggy from Finnegan's livery stable and show up at our farm with a big bouquet of roses or a heart-shaped box of fancy chocolates.

Throcky sure impressed Ma and Nettie real good, and even Pa figured the guy would be a good catch for Kate, who was sort of an old maid at 21. She gave in to the pressure and set the date as the second Sunday in June. Throcky went delirious with joy. He bought Sis a gold ring with a big, fat diamond in it. It cost more than a good team of horses and had all the single girls in town green with envy when she wore it to church. Somehow, though, she looked more like she was going to a funeral than to her wedding.

The problem was Snicker. Kate simply adored that horse. She'd go to his stall to brush and comb him until he fairly glowed. Then she'd mount him bareback without even a bridle and ride him wildly with her red hair a-streaming in the breeze, using just her knees to guide him. When she came in after these dashes, her eyes would be wet. Sometimes she'd cry on Ma's shoulder and go to her room without supper.

Well, the big day came, bright and sunny. Pa, Ma and the two girls and me, all slicked up in our Sunday clothes, were in our best buggy for the ride to the church. Kate wore the flouncy white dress Ma had been slaving over for weeks. She looked like she was going to a hanging.

As we passed the field where Snicker was grazing, he ran alongside our buggy, nickering like his heart would break. When he got to the end of the field, he hung his head over the fence and kept calling until we were out of sight.

Kate couldn't bear to look at him. She buried her face in her handkerchief and sobbed wildly.

There was a big crowd gathered on the church lawn as we stepped out in style. Women were *oohing* and *aahing* over Kate's dress, and men were shaking hands. What a turnout!

Suddenly there was bedlam on Main Street. As the crowd pulled back in squawking confusion, Snicker dashed up to a halt in front of Sis. His sides heaving, sweat streaming from every pore, he rubbed his nose on Kate's arm.

Kate put her arms around his neck in a big bear hug as Ma shrieked, "Your dress, Kathleen! You've ruined your lovely dress!" Folks came boiling out of the church to join the circle around Kate and her horse.

She tucked the engagement ring into his vest pocket.

Then Throcky was gently pulling her arms from Snicker. "Come now, my love," he urged. "We agreed you would give up your childish fondness for this dumb animal. It's time you came to your senses."

"I *have* come to my senses, Harrison," she said. "It wouldn't be any good for me to be cooped up in the city, and I'd miss Snicker too much." She tucked the engagement ring into his vest pocket. "I hope you'll understand."

Throcky didn't understand. He took a firm hold on her arm as if he would drag her into the church. Ma and some old busybodies started in on Sis about how she was betrothed.

They had her convinced when Snicker saw how things were going. He laid back his ears, bared his teeth and charged, scattering the group like chickens. Grabbing Throcky by his suit, he tossed him aside into the arms of his mother, who had come waddling to the rescue. "You are well rid of this hoyden, darling," she snapped. "Come; we must go back to civilization."

Throcky and some ladies thought they could mend things, but Sis led Snicker to the street, grabbed his mane and scrambled aboard. Her hair, streaming in the breeze, waved goodbye.

Ma and Pa were peeved at Kate, but they got over it when she up and married Jake Purdy soon afterward. I think he liked Snicker almost as much as Kate did.

One day I remarked to Jake how lucky it was for all concerned that Snicker had got out of this pasture that day in time to stop the wedding, though I did not see how he could do it.

"Wal, he jest kept a-workin' at the gate 'til he got it open," he grinned. "Of course, he might have got jest a *leetle* help from yours truly!" ❖

—Originally published in July 1986.

Things I Never Knew

By Patricia Happel Cornwell

As an ambitious career woman, I always thought of my business-owner father as my primary role model. As a child, I dreamed not of being a mommy in an ivy-covered cottage but of owning my own business.

My mother and I have always been good friends—except for a brief period when I was an obnoxious teenager and confided only in my horse—but for years, I have been unable to put my finger on exactly what my mother's legacy has been.

Finally, I decided to make a list of things my mother had imparted to me. (One of the things she taught me was to make lists.) As I sat smiling, thinking about life "at Mother's knee," some wonderfully important lessons became obvious.

My mother never preached (except to repeat "If there's one thing I can't stand, it's a liar!"), but the powerful principle of osmosis prevailed. Mother taught my brother and me what was important simply by living her life in full view of our young eyes. I wonder if my mother knows she taught me:

—To "make do" with my brother's hand-me-down shirts, with blackberries to fill a pie, with a refrigerator crate for a spaceship.

—To never go to town in curlers.

—To be a lady.

—To make jam if life hands you washtubs of ripe grapes or an acre of strawberries too ripe for market.

—To regard breakfast as a hot meal.

—To value family above possessions.

—To finish what I start.

—To sing out loud when I'm happy.

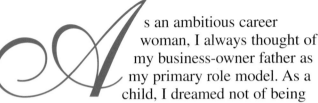

—To "pray like mad" when things go wrong.

—To work as hard as it takes. To stay married, to make a home, to pay the bills.

—To tuck in my child with a kiss every night, without fail.

—To never give up. Most of all, on myself.

I can't say my mother was tireless. When I was small, she was always pale and exhausted. But she was never too tired to fry the fish we kids caught, never too tired to find the candles so we could play dominoes when the lights went out, never too tired to curl my hair for church on Sunday. She never said, "Be a hard worker." She didn't have to.

A weak woman would have given up during the year of 20,000 baby chicks, two children, a menagerie of farm animals, ripening crops of tomatoes, strawberries and corn, and a husband who was out of town five days a week. A weak woman would have moved back to the city when the cows broke down the fence and went visiting, or when the well went dry, or when the mortgages on the farm and the business came due at the same time. But when she was 20 years old, she had said "for better or for worse" to an equally stubborn young man, and she meant it.

Nearly twenty years ago, my mother had surgery for cancer. We all grieved, but she kept her cheery disposition. "If you expect the worst, that's what you get," she'd say. Now she is healthier than she has ever been in her life, enjoying retirement with my father.

She's no quitter, this mother of mine. She never stops smiling. And she has no idea how much she has taught me about life. ❖

—Originally published in August 1986.

The Other Barber

By Maxine S. Nicholson

Deceit, I was taught, was first cousin to a lie. Truth, in our family, was such a valued commodity that the word *lie* was never mentioned in our presence. It ranked with such an unmentionable as *belly*. To be sure, Mother questioned us so closely that a lie, if it were even half-formed, would fold its wings and slip away. To deceive was just as bad. Half-truths or deceits could hurt a person's reputation even more than a lie. If it had a grain of truth in it, it could do more damage. On such is gossip built, and our mother hated gossip, so I knew better.

In those days, barbershops were the province of the men. In our town, matrons, schoolteachers and old maids still wore their hair long. Most of them, like Mother, twisted their hair in a knot on top of their heads. My teacher braided hers and fashioned a soft bun over each ear, indicating, I suppose, that she had attained maturity, as befitted a teacher, but was still

available for matrimony. The young ladies and the children, boys and girls wore short hair, but their use of the barbershops was limited to afternoons and Saturday mornings.

On those occasions when my sister led me, after much protest and tears, to our barber, he would lift me up onto the board he had placed across the arms of the barber chair, crank the chair up, flourish a long white cape in front of me, then tie it around my neck.

That barber knew me for a wriggling, squealing bit of humanity. He cupped my jaw gently in his hand and began to cut. This maneuver cut off my view of my reflection in the gleaming mirrors. I could just see the razor strop dangling from the side of the chair as he swung me around to snip each side. I squeezed my eyes shut as he trimmed my bangs, and giggled and scrunched up my shoulders when he buzzed the clippers around my neck.

We had three barbers in town, all on Main Street. There was a genteel black man who shaved and cut the hair of white men—no young ladies, no children and no other black people. There was Mr. Allen, our barber. Then there was another barber, new in town, whom we children designated The Other Barber.

That was the situation until my sister Ruth decided to learn to cut hair. Our parents encouraged us to learn to do things, so we all suffered through Gladys' gritty greens, my purple socks, and Ruth's short bout with the scissors. I was her first and last victim. What with my wriggling and Ruth's inexperience with scissors and clippers, I was a sight to behold.

The next day at school, the kids gathered around. "Who cut your hair?"

I bowed my head and told my lie: The Other Barber."

The Other Barber didn't last long in our town. I have often wondered in shame if, in my half-lie, I helped ruin his reputation. ❖

—Originally published in July 1987.

Not So Fast

By Mike Stephani

When does a boy become a man? My earliest, most vivid memory of my stumbling steps toward becoming a man occurred when I was 9 years old.

Every summer, my father put up the wild hay in what we called the meadow; the ground was much too wet and rough to be called a field. But we needed the hay, so the work had to be done. In dry years, putting up the meadow hay wasn't too bad. The horses could pull the mower without much trouble. But in wet years, they could step into soft spots and break legs. If horses couldn't cut the hay, then people had to do it.

As a child, cutting the meadow was an exciting time because I could sit on the side and watch the horses and men work. There is a clarity, even after 46 years, to the memories of watching my father's horses work. In my mind, the sky is always vivid blue with floating white cumulus clouds, and the grass is bright, wind-blown green. Silhouetted against the sky and grass is one black horse with his brown partner, leaning into their collars as they pulled the mower through grass higher than my head.

While watching the horses was prime entertainment, my greatest joy was watching the hired men. With deceivingly easy grace, they cut the grass next to the small river with a scythe. Their broad backs and shoulders, always bare and glistening with sweat in the late-July heat, rippled with muscles that any skinny child would envy. One swing of a scythe and a great swathe of meadow grass fell.

On this day, I lay in impotent rage in the shade with lunch kits and water bottles. I was big and strong enough to help my dad make hay! Earlier, I had pleaded with one of the hired men to let me use his scythe, but he, as did most of the men, had laughed at me. "Wait till you grow up, Sonny," was his only reply.

As the morning passed, I grew more and more morose. Soon there would be no grass left for me to cut. During lunch, the men's laughter and jokes about my wanting to use a man-sized tool didn't help my mood.

After they finished eating, they went down to the river to take a quick cooling-off dip before returning to work.

I saw my chance. Right by the curve of the river stood a strip of uncut emerald green grass. A scythe was lying there, waiting for me. I looked around. The men were far enough off to pay no attention to me. Grasping the opportunity and the scythe, I set to work cutting hay. I thought that after I had cut the grass, my father would have to admit I was a man who could work alongside him and the hired hands.

The hay went down easily. Then the master stroke, the clearest memory of all. There, right in the middle of my swing, which I couldn't stop, was the largest hornet's nest I have ever seen. Watching the blade, whose arc I couldn't control, go dead for the middle of that monstrous nest is a memory of nightmares. Each blade of grass with its sparkle of moisture and each hornet with its blur of wing is etched with camera sharpness—as was the sharpness of the stings biting into my face and bare chest.

Though a moment before I had seen no one close to me, within seconds, I felt strong arms grasp me and throw me in the air. With a splash, refreshingly cool water surrounded me. My dad's voice came: "Swim downstream and the hornets will leave you. Duck under if you have to!"

At least I had the sense to do what he told me. When I had gone a hundred or so feet, the hornets had left me—but from the way I hurt, I'm not sure it made any difference. The earlier sharpness of vision was gone behind eyes swollen shut almost too tightly for tears to escape.

As I crawled out of the stream into my dad's arms, I said what to him must have seemed crazy words: "Dad, I don't think I like being a man." ❖

—Originally published in August 1987.

The Rodeo Rider

By J.B. Cearley

The angry August sun was really bearing down that hot, dusty Friday in 1933. I had been glancing at the sun for an hour, wondering if the old rascal we were hoeing cotton for would ever let us quit. Finally, the old man looked at his watch and turned to say, "Well, boys, I 'spect we can call it a day. It's 6:30." My older brother and I had been cutting weeds since 7 o'clock that morning. We had been working all week to earn cash for school clothes. The old man stopped, stalling for time before he gave us our pay. We had him pegged as a greedy old goat who worked boys for half what he should pay.

He turned to face us like a judge ready to pass sentence. "Let me see, you boys worked five days. At $1.25 a day, that figures out to a whopping $6.25 each. You boys gettin' rich!"

Finally, the old man gave us our pay for working 65 hours chopping weeds. He felt he had done us a favor. We both said thanks and that we would be back next week to finish his cotton field.

Chad Wilson walked by and asked, "You boys riding today?"

We got our pay and started walking a mile and a half home. "What you going to do with your pay?" I asked my brother.

"I need to buy a pair of decent shoes. I also need pants and shirts. It would be nice if we could go to the rodeo in Tahoka tomorrow. I was afraid old Roper would demand that we hoe on Saturday, too. Boy, we need a day off."

"I think he needed the day of rest," I said. "We had the old fool worked down. He was ready to quit two hours ago."

Once home, we had to milk our seven cows and feed the hogs and steers Dad was fattening for sale. I was dog-tired when we got through. I was relaxing with one foot on the bottom board of the large corral when Dad walked by. He paused and asked, "How'd you boys like to go to the rodeo at the county seat tomorrow?"

"That would be nice," I said.

Brother walked up and heard us. "You bet!" he said. "I want to see the rodeo. Maybe we could stop in town and I could look for shoes. I need decent shoes to wear to church."

"Then we'll go tomorrow," Dad promised.

Saturday started off like a banner of a day. For one thing, we got to sleep an extra hour that was much needed after all that weed chopping. While we boys and Dad did the milking and feeding of the stock, Mom was cooking breakfast: hot biscuits, butter, scrambled eggs, crisp fried bacon strips, coffee, cold milk, and two kinds of berry jam. That breakfast made a kid feel good.

About midmorning, we got into the Model A to ride 15 miles to Tahoka. The folks sold their eggs and cream while Brother and I looked at the stores for clothes we could afford.

For lunch, we got to stop at a small restaurant and eat Texas chili. We felt like rich kids instead of country hicks.

At midafternoon, we drove out to the fairgrounds for the rodeo. A crowd was gathering, folks from the farms and ranches. The town wasn't much—only 2,500 people. It was a typical West Texas town during the Dust Bowl days.

A few minutes later, Chad Wilson walked by and asked, "You boys riding today?"

"Me?" I was startled. "No, not in the rodeo."

"I'm going to try the bareback horse riding," Chad said.

"Good luck," I said. Chad might do well since his dad had a ranch in the mesquite brakes. They rode horses every day, and Chad was 18.

The announcer called the crowd to attention, and the rodeo began with a bang. First out of the chute was a wild bull with a frightened rider on its back.

The angry bull made two leaps and shied sideways. The cowboy rolled into the dirt. He got to his feet as the crowd cheered. Then the bull turned and made a dash at the cowpoke. Luckily, one of the rodeo clowns scared the bull away from the addled boy.

It was exciting watching most of the country boys get bucked off their bulls and horses. Chad did very well and won $25 for his ride. I thought a lot about that. He had been on that horse only 15 seconds and made what I could earn in a month cutting weeds for old Roper.

The rodeo ended, and we rode back to town so the folks could purchase our grocery supply. Then it was time to head back to the farm and do the evening chores.

Sunday afternoon, brother and I were sitting on the big porch, trying to rest and beat the heat. Brother said, "You ought to learn to ride a bull or a bronc. Old Chad made a lot of money."

"Yeah," I agreed, "I'll never get rich cutting weeds. I could probably hang on a bull for 10 or 15 seconds."

"For 25 bucks, that would be over a hundred dollars an hour. Now, that's real money!"

I should have known what he was up to, but he was a sly one and always figuring out something for me to do. Since he was older by two years, I often let him get me into big trouble.

A cowboy rides a steer in a rodeo in Wagon Mound, N.M., in September 1939. Photograph by Russell Lee courtesy of the Library of Congress, FSA-OWI Collection.

He said easily, "Let's walk out to the corral."

I followed him out to the barns. We had what we called a large cow lot. On a ranch, it would have been called a corral. The lot was 50 yards square. A shed across the north opened on the south into the corral. We could pen all our livestock there during the winter months.

Brother spoke kindly. "You ought to practice riding that little brindle calf."

I turned to look at the mean critter. *Little?* That wild thing weighed over 800 pounds.

"I think I'll pass on that," I told brother.

"Coward." He said the word softly, with a lot of disgust. "I actually thought you were interested in making some real cash. Our baby brother could easily ride that little calf."

Baby Brother was 9 to my 14 years. Baby Brother wouldn't be caught in the pen with that wild steer. The thing ran wild in our Sudan pasture. He was no gentle calf.

Brother turned like he was walking away in disgust. "Well, if you have no interest in making a hundred bucks, maybe two, a week, then forget it. You said you were thinking of entering the rodeo, and I was merely going to help you get started on something real easy."

I glanced at the big steer. Then I spoke too proudly, "I'm going to make some big money—someday."

Brother faced me, speaking softly. "The time to start is right now." The next thing I knew, Brother had run that steer into the corral. "I'll fix you a rope cinch, then you can practice with this little gentle calf."

A few moments later, brother had the steer roped and made a girth of a small rope. The big brindle steer was standing there as nice as a kitten. "A kid could ride this calf," he insisted.

"I'm not quite ready," I said, stalling.

"Coward. My brother is a 'fraidy-cat. I'll be ashamed to tell people that you refused to ride this calf."

I looked at Brother, then at the giant steer. "I'm just not ready," I said, trying to back away.

He grabbed me by the arm and pulled me to the steer. "Get on there and show me how you can ride. I'll bet you can make a bundle of cash at the rodeos."

Somehow, he got me astride the critter. I caught the cinch and was ready to bite the dust, but the calf just stood there like a gentle lamb.

Brother took his hat and slapped the steer in the flanks. Wow! That steer jumped 20 feet. When he hit the ground, my teeth rattled. Then that steer raced wildly toward that shed, made a quick turn and streaked to the west end of the long shed. Then he raced around the corral at 20 miles an hour. He was picking up speed—and hatred for the thing on his back. The faster he ran, the more he bucked. I was ready to alight, but no one had told me how I could get

off. I clung to the rope, praying that the steer wouldn't kill me.

That critter shifted into high gear for this third circle around the lot, doing about 60, I thought. He kept bucking so that my head was flopping back and forth. "Hang on!" Brother called. "You're doing fine!"

Suddenly I felt the rope break. Now I had nothing with which to hold on to that bucking steer. He shifted into overdrive, and he fairly flew around the lot. He raced under the shed, made a quick turn and headed west, doing 70!

A seizure of panic swept over me as I saw that west wall. I just knew that the steer would crash into the wall, and I would be killed. But the steer had other plans. As he neared the wall, he made a square turn and raced into the lot. I, however, failed to turn with him. I went airborne and kept flying, straight into the side of the shed, doing 75!

The big brindle steer was standing there as nice as a kitten. "A kid could ride this calf," he insisted.

For a few seconds, I thought I was entering the Pearly Gates. I saw a million stars, and everything was whirling around. I heard the loud crash and thought I had landed in my heavenly abode. A minute later, I rolled over and opened one eye. It was then that I saw the hole I had made in the barn. I had knocked off two 12-inch boxing planks before plowing into the ground with my face.

Dad walked by, stopped and said, "You trying to tear down the shed, Son? Better get some nails and the hammer and put those boards back in place." As he walked away, I could see that he was chuckling about my wild ride.

I managed to sit up as Brother walked over to see about me. I was relieved that no bones were broken. Brother was laughing as he said, "You did all right. Want to enter the rodeo next Saturday? Make a lot of money?"

"No, thanks," I told him. "I like cutting weeds in a dusty cotton field too much for fooling with a rodeo."

That was my first and last experience at bull riding. ❖

—Originally published in February 1988.

Facing page: *Good Old Days* magazine cover, February 1988, House of White Birches nostalgia archives

DISPLAY UNTIL JANUARY 26

$1.50 $2.00 CANADA

b 47312

THE MAGAZINE THAT REMEMBERS THE BEST

GOOD·OLD·DAYS

FEBRUARY, 1988

Those Precious
Moments of Love
Revisited

Return With Us to the
Yesteryear of the
Cowboy

John Slobodnik

FEATURING STORIES ❖ PHOTOS ❖ ILLUSTRATIONS
of the Happy Days Gone By

Hypnotizing Gramp's Cow

By Gertrude Harrington

My gramp's farm was just down the road from my house. It had a rambling white farmhouse with a huge screened porch, an old weathered hay barn and a red rambling cow barn with another hay barn attached to that. It was a wonderful place to play hide-and-seek or cops and robbers. My cousins and I knew every secret hiding place in each barn. Our summer days were spent there.

One particular day stands out in my memory. Annie and I were trailing along behind the cows, wishing they would hurry. Dart, the dog, nipped at their heels. We were anxious to get there because in my pocket was a very important box that the mailman had delivered.

After we reached the pasture that bordered the woods and the cows were contentedly grazing, Annie and I quickly opened our secret box. In it was the most beautiful pendant that we had ever seen! The long chain was made of the richest gold, and the crystal was as big as a walnut. When we held it up to the sunlight, it reflected all the colors of the rainbow.

Our magic crystal pendant was in our very own hands, we could just feel the power of mystery stirring within us. It was even more beautiful than the picture on the comic book had shown. There was no doubt about it. It must have belonged to a real gypsy!

Annie and I quickly read the instructions. They were simple enough. All we had to do was find a willing subject who would like to be hypnotized, try to make him relax, and then dangle our magic pendant before his eyes while we counted slowly in a monotone voice. Then, once our subject was under our spell, we should be able to get him to obey our every command.

I volunteered to be the subject. I followed Annie's directions to the letter, but somehow I just couldn't fall asleep.

Next, I tried my mystical powers on Annie, but to no avail. We sat on the stone wall, wondering where we had failed. Certainly anything that cost 59 cents could not be fake!

As I sat lamenting, I dangled the pendant in the sunlight and watched the beautiful colors reflecting from its prisms. Suddenly Annie and I were aware that we were not the only ones admiring the crystal. There stood Arabella, Gramp's favorite cow, staring intently at the magical crystal as she stood there, grazing. There was no doubt about it. Arabella was in a trance! We were thrilled to pieces. We had known all the time that we possessed mystical powers, and now our proof stood numbly before us.

We tried to give her a few simple commands, but with no results. Nevertheless, we were not discouraged by Arabella's lack of cooperation. After all, how many cows knew enough to obey a command at *any* time, awake or asleep? The rest of the day, Annie and I basked in the glory of our first success in the field of hypnotism.

When 3 o'clock came, we started to round up the cows. Dart barked his usual commands and all the cows headed toward the gate—all, that is, except Arabella! Dart nipped at her heels, but she refused to budge an inch. Annie spoke to her softly while I pushed the old cow's rump. Still she stood without

moving a muscle. I tried to coax her by dangling the magic pendant in front of her eyes while I walked backward to the gate, but still she stood rooted to the ground. We pleaded with her, bribed her with grass, and even cuffed her with a stick. But no matter what we tried, Arabella just stood there, transfixed!

By now, our feelings of elation had evaporated. In fact, we were darned scared. What was our grandfather going to say when we returned without his cow? And what would happen if he found out what we had done to her?

Finally, as we couldn't put it off any longer, we started back to the barn without Arabella. Just as soon as we headed the cows into their stanchions, Gramp started roaring that we'd lost his prize cow. We quickly told him that Arabella didn't seem to be up to her old self, and that she had stubbornly refused to come back. Gramp set out on a dead run to the north pasture with his hired hand trailing behind.

Two hours later, the trio returned. Gramps looked bewildered, the hired hand was shaking his head, and old Arabella was looking as normal as could be. We watched as they tied her up in the barn. She certainly appeared to have returned to her old self, much to our relief.

That evening, as we pretended to be sleeping on the cots on the porch, we heard Gramp telling Gram about Arabella's strange behavior. It seemed that the old girl had simply stood for close to two hours without moving. Then, suddenly, as if she remembered something, she up and headed straight for the barn.

Gram, after hearing this story, was positive that the cow had been into the green apples again. Gramp felt sure that she had been bit by some rare type of wood tick. When the veterinarian examined her the next morning, he announced that he was sure that the cow had suffered sunstroke.

Only Annie and I knew the real truth—and we didn't dare tell! ❖

—Originally published in May 1988.

DISPLAY UNTIL APRIL 19

THE MAGAZINE THAT REMEMBERS THE BEST

$1.50

B 47312

GOOD · OLD · DAYS

MAY, 1988

How We Made May Baskets

Bits and Pieces Of Her Heart

FEATURING STORIES ❖ PHOTOS ❖ ILLUSTRATIONS of the Happy Days Gone By

Cast-Iron Mailbox

By Robert L. Tefertillar

*H*ey Rip, what do you think would happen if I dropped this 2-incher in that mailbox?"

"Probably make a dandy sound, and yet it just might put a crack in it. You know your grandma is mighty proud of that new mailbox."

"Let's try it with a lady finger and see what happens," I suggested.

"Yeah, a little firecracker couldn't possibly hurt it, and we would have some idea of what a bigger one would do."

I opened the top of the massive, black, cast-iron box and tossed the tiny, fuse-sputtering firecracker inside. There was a small *pop!* and wisps of satisfying smoke snaked out the sides of the undamaged mailbox.

"Boy, I sure would like to use this 2-incher to see what it would sound like going off in that mailbox!" I mused.

"Better not. We can get some more old tin cans and put big firecrackers under them and watch them fly into the air," Rip grunted.

"Some kid dropped a firecracker in your mailbox and blew it to pieces."

We did, but the curiosity of what a big firecracker would do in that mailbox was becoming an obsession with me.

In the late 1930s, fireworks were legal in Illinois, and we kids considered July Fourth the second best holiday of all—Halloween being our favorite.

We started the action early by shooting some of our precious fireworks a week before the Fourth. The practice of putting a firecracker under a tin can and then running like the dickens was pure entertainment. The only problem was getting the money for firecrackers to provide such sport.

I earned my money working Saturdays at Morgan's grocery store, candling eggs and filling the local farmers' grocery orders. The rural families would come to town early Saturday morning, leave their grocery lists to be filled, then leave to do other shopping and take in a movie.

The movies didn't end till around 10 p.m., and we working youngsters would wait till the last farm family picked up their supplies and headed for home. That's when we were paid our $3 and dreamed of Monday, when we could buy cherry bombs, sparklers, snakes, sky rockets, fountains and the ultimate: firecrackers in various sizes and explosive power.

July 4, 1939, dawned a perfect day for kids. It was hot and sunshiny with only a few white clouds floating in the sky. I met Rip under the buckeye tree next to the summer kitchen.

"Rip, I've been thinking about it for a week, and I just gotta see what his 2-incher will do to that mailbox."

"Man, I've wondered about it, too. But, if it should happen to crack it, your grandpa will really tan you good," Rip wisely reminded me.

"I don't think it will. I just think there will be a tremendous explosion and smoke will shoot out of that thing. It will be a heck of a lot better than seeing a tin can pop up in the air."

I lit the fuse, opened the lid and dropped the big firecracker into the mailbox. That sucker *exploded* and blew the cast-iron mailbox to smithereens! "Crime-a-netley!" Rip screamed. "Now look at what you have done!"

I stood, shell-shocked, in a horrified stupor. "Well, you said it might be OK," I managed to sputter. "Besides, we can say some other kid did it."

"You handle it any way you want. I'm taking off before your grandma comes out!"

Rip mounted his trusty black-and-white Hawthorne bike and sped away, leaving me in the midst of shattered pieces of black cast iron with no explanation as to how the mailbox had been totally destroyed.

I hadn't seen my faithful dog, Pepper, for a week—not since the firecrackers started popping. Pepper hated the Fourth of July as much as he loved Halloween. He now slunk out from under the front porch, tail between his legs, giving me a reproachful look.

"Hey, Pepper, you seen Beans do it, didn't you, old buddy?" I hopefully cried knowing Pepper would back me to the bitter end. For the first time, he looked at me with disdain and scurried under the summer kitchen, his safest hide-away.

The bomb wasn't dropped until supper that evening. Grandpa pushed his plate back and addressed Grandma. "Some fool kid dropped a firecracker in your new mailbox and blew it to pieces."

"What?" Grandma shrieked. "It had to be that roughneck friend of Bobbie's, Rip. I'll go over and see his mother after dishes and make sure he gets his comeuppance."

I sat in guilty, cowardly silence. How could I possibly let Rip take the blame? There was no way I could—but I did.

The next time I saw Rip was a rainy, soggy day a few days later. We met under the buckeye tree, and he greeted me in stony, accusing silence.

"Uh, hey, Rip … how you doing?" I asked, not daring to look him in the eyes.

"You know dang well how I'm doing." Rip muttered in a soft, angry undertone. "I took a heck of a razor stroppin' for you, Bobbie, and we ain't never gonna be best friends, ever, anymore. But I didn't snitch on you!"

Guilt hit me in the stomach like a physical blow. "Well, uh, Rip, I, you see, I …"

Rip didn't bother to listen. He just turned his back and strode away. I thought I saw a tear glisten in his eye as a remembrance of our past friendship, but it was probably only a stray raindrop.

I worried and fretted in my dilemma for a week, even to the point that Grandma put me to bed, fearing I was really ill. Any boy my age that wasn't fishing or swimming in the creek, playing cowboy and Indians with the gang, had to have something drastically wrong. I wasn't eating, sleeping or feeling well, and finally I couldn't stand it any longer. One evening at the supper table, I just blurted it out.

"Rip didn't blow up that mailbox, Grandma, I did. He just took the blame for me!"

I could not believe it, but no matter what the consequences of my confession, a blessed relief came over me. My appetite returned, and I felt better than I had for a week.

Grandpa was judge, jury and executioner in our household, and I waited for him to deliver sentence, with level eyes, a clear conscience and unbowed head. "Bobbie, how much you saved up from working at the grocery store this summer?" he grated.

"'Bout $5," I truthfully replied. "But I been saving it for that new jackknife I want something awful."

"Five dollars is just about right for a new mailbox. You give it all to your Grandma. You don't get no more movies, comic books, treats, swimming, fishing, that new knife, or riding your bike the rest of the summer. How you make it up to Rip is strictly up to you." The judgment passed, Grandpa headed for the front porch swing.

Rip had gotten off easy; this sentence was harsh. Fall was an eternity away, and the privileges denied me, plus the loss of my dream knife, were my favorite summer things to do. However, I still felt better than I had since the Fourth of July.

Well, Rip heard about my confession (and he told me later it was from my grandpa, of all people), and we became best friends again. We didn't see much of one another the rest of the summer, though; he was off bike riding, swimming or fishing with the rest of the gang. I was grounded to my yard except for the days I had to work at Morgan's.

My regular household chores included chopping kindling, hauling in coal morning and evening, keeping the kitchen water pail filled and trudging down the lane each evening to pick up the mail. This was the easiest task—and the one I hated most!

Ever since that fateful July Fourth blunder, I despised going after the mail. That massive, cast-iron black box seemed to grin at me when I opened its awesome maw to stick in my hand for the envelopes, catalogs and newspapers.

I always hurriedly pulled my hand from inside, skinning my knuckles and constantly pinching my fingers in opening and shutting its smirking mouth.

That was probably the worst, and the best, summer I ever had. Oh, by the way, I got my new, coveted jackknife as a Christmas present from Grandpa. ❖

—Originally published in July 1988.

My Only Piano Recital

By Doris Burville

*I*n spite of the fact that I had 10 thumbs unfit for any task more exacting than shelling peas, Mama had hopes I would learn to play the piano. A lot of farmers had pianos or pump organs that they had lugged over hill and dale from back East, and most hadn't been tuned for years.

But farm women would limber up their work-stiffened fingers and plunk out songs, paying no mind to the fact their piano was off-key. They played hymns mostly, but Mama would liven things up with popular songs of her day, which my crabby old cousin Mamie called "shameless."

And so, 10 thumbs or not, I had to have lessons. Mama was bent on "encouraging my musical tendency."

Every Saturday at 11 a.m. on the dot, Miz Appleby clattered up our road in her one-horse buggy to teach me scales. Miz Appleby never criticized the off-key piano; and she only sighed when I struck a sour note. She managed to teach me *Kitten on the Keys* and *Glow Worm*, and when I got the hang of *In a Country Garden*, I was qualified for her "Budding Artistes Piano Recital."

After every lesson, Mamie would wail, "The child's got no ear for music." But I knew better. Couldn't I beat out the tunes of every Sousa march the Grange band played every Sunday in the park—with my toes? I did *so* have an ear for music—and I would prove it at the recital!

On the big day, we students sat, stiff as frozen long johns on the line, waiting for our turn to display our talents while proud relatives squirmed on Miz Appleby's horsehair settees or chairs borrowed from O'Del's Funeral Parlor.

Zeke Barker was first on the program, and with ears as red as a rooster's comb, he clumped to the piano and banged out an ear-splitting rendition of *Asleep in the Deep*. Then he slunk to his seat, looking as though he hoped the floor would open and swallow him whole.

Nettie Nussbaum sashayed up, starched skirts crackling, an oversized bow fastened to her corkscrew curls. Her piece was *Beautiful Ohio*, gussied up with a lot of tinkles that made a big hit with the audience.

I was the last of seven on the program, and I darted to the piano, wiped my palms on my dress and struck the first notes of *In a Country Garden*. From the corner of my eye, I saw folks sway to the old, familiar tune, and it made me proud.

Everything was going fine until I hit keys that had a strange ring to them. This piano didn't sound like ours at home. My *Country Garden* was turning into a weed patch under my slowly petrifying fingers.

All thumbs again, I began to hit the wrong keys, and while Nettie snickered and the audience murmured pitying sounds, I slid into my chair and prayed the floor would open so I could join Zeke in the swallow-up.

I heard cousin Mamie sniff her usual I-told-you-so sniff, and I knew she would natter all the way home about my "tin ear." But I also knew what the trouble was, and it wasn't me. It was the piano! Miz Appleby's piano was in tune! ❖

—Originally published in August 1988.

The Decision

By Margaret Newton

Bread was browning in the oven, filling the small house tucked at the foot of Mount Baker with a homey fragrance on this winter day in 1936. It was a beautiful day. The sun was shining, and a soft sifting of snowflakes was falling, laying a glaze of white icing on the earth.

Papa had ridden his horse down the mountain that morning to Baker, Ore., to work in the sawmill, carrying with him eggs to sell to the townsfolk.

My mother and father had lost a small son last winter when he had fallen into an old covered well on his way home from school. His pictures, along with his clay marbles and other keepsakes, had been put away in the big black trunk that sat in Mama and Papa's bedroom. The trunk contained wedding photos and graduation, marriage, birth and death certificates—forbidden treasures we children were not allowed to touch without adult supervision.

My sister Ruth and I were not old enough to go to school, but our sister Shirley, an envied first-grader, had left for the small, one-room country school about a mile from our house.

Around noon, the soft placid snowflakes whirled white against the gray sky. Suddenly, without warning, the wind and snow increased, and the sky turned black. Mama was afraid Shirley might have left school before the storm had hit. She reasoned that the teacher had kept the children at school, but she couldn't know that for sure. She knew Papa would not make it back up the mountain that night.

She alone must decide: Should she leave two little ones alone and go after Shirley? With God's help, she quickly made her decision. She piled more wood in the stove, hoping it would keep us warm until morning if she couldn't get back to us. Then, to our disbelief, she pulled out the trunk, opened the lid and told us we could look at everything in it.

She pulled Papa's thick wool mackinaw, galoshes, mittens and a shawl over her head. Then, telling us she might not be back for a long time, she closed the door. We watched as she fought the wind across the yard to reach the rail fence. Moving hand over hand, she was out of sight in seconds.

We rushed back to the trunk and plowed into the contents, with no fear that Mama might not come back. Mama always came back.

She found Shirley not far from school, holding on to the fence, waist-deep in snow, just waiting. She knew Mama would come.

Mama picked her up and tried to carry her, but soon saw that that was not going to work. They must hold on to the fence or be lost. She tied one end of the shawl around Shirley and the other end around herself. Slowly they headed for home. All the way, Mama prayed that the little ones she had left alone were safe.

Hours had passed, but the wonderful treasures in the trunk kept us occupied. Before we reached the bottom, Mama and Shirley walked in the door. Mama was calm as she re-dressed Shirley in dry clothes. Then she sat down in the rocker, gathered the three of us to her and cried. We wondered what was wrong with Mama. We weren't worried. Her tears turned to laughter when Shirley wanted her turn in the trunk.

Of course, she got it. ❖

—Originally published in January 1989.

Never Touch The Winchester

By Gen Moore

Great-Grandfather Henry hailed originally from the Blue Ridge country of Virginia. He was born and reared there, but as a young man, began a homesteading trek all the way from Virginia to the Wyoming line.

He was a true pioneer. Whenever another family settled within a mile of him, at once he felt crowded and would move to new territory. He took his last homestead in western Nebraska at the age of 70 with his faithful wife, two grown bachelor sons, and a pack of hound dogs that, in Grandfather's eyes, were just as important as the human members of his household.

One evening, the dogs chased a bobcat up onto the roof of the sod house. It had been built against a range of hills north of the old man's ranch. The dogs

rushed around, yelping at the cat, which was now making unhappy yowling noises as it perched above them.

Hearing the bedlam, Grandfather ran up from the corrals and sighted the bobcat. Immediately he hurried into the house after his Winchester, which was always in one corner of the living room, loaded and ready to go. But this evening, it wasn't there. Grandmother had been cleaning, sweeping, dusting, shaking the bearskin rug and rearranging the clutter.

Grandfather yelled for Grandmother. He upset things all over the house searching for his weapon, even looking in the kitchen cupboard. By the time Grandmother came in from the yard and found the gun behind the flour barrel, the cat had vanished. It had jumped from the roof and disappeared into the brush.

The dogs were running here and there in the yard, sniffing around the lean-to with an injured and baffled air. Grandfather had to go back into the soddy without even firing a shot.

Seeing Grandmother in the kitchen, he proceeded in his customary fashion to speak his mind to her. "Olive, hereafter you are to confine your housekeeping activities to the kitchen pots and pans and your own belongings, and never, never, *never* touch the Winchester!" Grandmother listened impassively.

From then on, the gun was always in its rightful place in the living room corner, along with an assortment of Grandfather's riding boots, bridles, cleaning rods and plain junk. It all gathered dust and grime without any interference on Grandmother's part.

Whenever someone loitered to stare at the mess, she would always smile and say, "You know, I never touch the Winchester." ❖

—Originally published in February 1989.

Bottom of the Dad-Dratted Matter

By Robert G. Tucker

*I*n June 1945, the German high command had just surrendered in Europe; the imperial Japanese forces would throw in the towel before the summer was over; and the Rev. Orrin B. Snum's annual strawberry festival was demolished by a minor blitzkrieg. My tag-along 10-year-old brother, Rusty, and my best pal, Tom Cheever, and I couldn't take any credit for the Axis armies' losing ways, but we sure masterminded the bombardment of the poor preacher's ill-fated strawberry fete. Tom was 13 that summer, and I was about a year younger.

Our plan was a masterpiece of simplicity. Half a package of Fourth of July cherry bombs, bought with pooled allowance money, were Scotch-taped together with their fuses wrapped around the base of a smoldering Old Gold cigarette. The "T-Bomb" (named in honor of Tom, who thought up the idea) was lighted and placed under a crepe-festooned table on the lawn of the Methodist church while the congregation was inside singing gospel hymns.

The delayed fuse gave us about a quarter of an hour to establish our alibis, and we took advantage of the time by going inside to be seen mingling innocently with the crowd.

The hymn-sing over, the lighthearted crowd adjourned to the church lawn where refreshments were spread out on the table directly over the ominously smoking cigarette fuse. Old Preacher Snum, roly-poly and unctuous as always, offered up a prayer for God's blessing upon the food. He was just about to cut into a huge strawberry chiffon cake when the T-Bomb went off—not with a single bang, but with a staccato series of explosions that sounded as if the Strawberry Festival were being strafed. And from the crowd's reaction, you would have sworn that a rogue Luftwaffe pilot was indeed taking out his frustration over the Nazi defeat upon the Methodists of Hampton Falls, N.H.

People screamed and ran. The refreshment table collapsed, dumping the beautiful strawberry chiffon cake and a huge bowl of strawberry punch onto the grass. The deacons, dour Wesleyans all,

DISPLAY UNTIL MAY 23
$1.95

THE MAGAZINE THAT REMEMBERS THE BEST

GOOD·OLD·DAYS

SWEET AND FRAGRANT MAKE ROSE POTPOURRI

JUNE 1989

ENDURING SECRETS OF A HAPPY MARRIAGE

K 47312

THE IRREPRESSIBLE
Ma Kettle

FEATURING STORIES ♦ PHOTOS ♦ ILLUSTRATIONS
of the Happy Days Gone By

ran about like frantic squirrels, trying vainly to identify the perpetrators of the horrendous deed.

They came up with several possibilities, including boys from the Congregational church across the town common, but Tom and Rusty and I were not among the suspects. We had pulled off the perfect crime. Or so we thought.

Tom Cheever and his mother ate dinner at our house that evening. After the meal, we all gathered around the venerable Emerson radio in the parlor. That's when my dog, a cocker spaniel named Prince, chose to amble in and drop a love offering between my feet for all to see. Prince's "gift" was the unused half package of Thunderclap cherry bombs that I had carefully hidden under my bed. The jig was up, and we all knew it.

Pa sighed. "So, that's how it is," he said. Then he arose, clicked the radio off and left the room. He returned after a moment, snapping a well-oiled razor strop against his right thigh. "Robbie, Rusty," he commanded, "we'll step out back to the woodshed, boys, where I'm fixing to get straight to the bottom of this dad-dratted matter."

Mrs. Cheever looked helplessly up at my father. "Oh, Dan," she said, "I'm not strong enough. Would you mind terribly?"

"Not at all, Alice. Fall in, Tom."

Feet dragging, we three miscreants began our interminable march to the woodshed. As I filed past Ma, I cast an angelic smile at her, but I received only a frown of disapproval in return.

"Take your pants off, guys," Pa said firmly, closing the woodshed door behind him and snapping on a fly-specked light bulb that dangled from the ceiling at the end of a frayed cord.

"Aw, Pa, we was only funnin'," my little brother asserted lamely.

"Is that a fact?" Pa stopped to help Rusty with his belt buckle, my brother's fingers having turned to rubber. "Step on out of your britches, son. This will remind you to set some limits next time you're tempted. You and I've been through this before, boy. You know what to do."

"Yes, sir," my brother sighed miserably. After hanging his white ducks on a nail, he moved a dilapidated straight-backed wooden

chair kept in the shed for just such occasions to the middle of the floor and jackknifed indecorously over the backrest, making a likely target of his puckered behind.

Pa proceeded to lay on seven vigorous spanks to the accompaniment of wall-shaking yowls of protest from Rusty. When it was over, my brother clutched his incandescent bottom and danced in tight circles around the floor, hollering at the top of his lungs and blowing out through clenched teeth.

And then Tom was bending over the chair and Pa was hoisting his shirttails. I leaned back against the woodshed wall and shook as my boyhood buddy got peppered 10 times by Pa's ferocious strop. Then, while Tom Cheever was whooping in anguish and doing his own fair imitation of a Comanche war dance, my father beckoned for me to present myself.

I approached the chair as if I were walking on eggshells. My bottom itched maddeningly. Grimly, I bent over the backrest and lifted my shirttails. Silver teardrops already glistened on the seat of the chair.

"Son, this will hurt me more 'n it hurts you," Pa assured me.

"I doubt it, sir," I answered honestly, gritting my teeth and screwing up my face muscles.

The licking was administered quickly, and it felt exactly as if a swarm of angry yellow jackets was attacking my bare fundament. When Pa was finished, even Rusty and Tom stopped yowling to stare at me in openmouthed awe and cover their ears to block out my lusty caterwauling.

That all happened nearly 45 years ago. Between our tail-whuppin's and having to get up in front of the congregation to apologize for our behavior, we three small, overly exuberant boys were miraculously toned down.

Nowadays, of course, the juvenile court would become involved—along with a passel of social workers and child psychiatrists, each one trying to analyze our patterns of repressed hostility. Pa's gone now, but if he were around, he could sure tell the experts how to get to the bottom of this dad-dratted matter. ❖

—Originally published in June 1989.

Feet dragging, we three miscreants began our interminable march to the woodshed.

THE MAGAZINE THAT REMEMBERS THE BEST

GOOD ✦ OLD ✦ DAYS ®

The Old Blue Range
Ye Olde Englishe Sanitation

January 1995

Radio Orphan Annie's
Secret Society Decoders

GOOD ✦ OLD ✦ DAYS

FEATURING STORIES ✦ PHOTOS ✦ ILLUSTRATIONS
Of the Happy Days Gone By

The '90s: Looking Back

Chapter Four

Janice and I had been with the magazine several years when I realized that our readers really wanted to know more about us. So, like the original editor of *Good Old Days*, Edward Kutlowski, I started writing a monthly column in May 1993 called "Looking Back."

Today the feature, one of the most popular in the magazine, continues to give us a way of returning a bit of the love our hundreds of thousands of readers have shown us.

Here is one of those early "Looking Backs," originally published in January 1995.

～

Back when I was growing up, I yearned to "stay up like the big kids do." That meant I wanted to push my bedtime just as late as I possibly could. I have no idea who those "big kids" were I always referred to when arguing my case to Mama and Daddy; my big brother, Dennis, five years my elder, had the same bedtime as I.

I'm sure my bedtime would seem tame. From my earliest memories it seems it was around 8 p.m. in the winter; in the summer it was as soon after sundown as Mama could get us inside, cleaned up and bedded down. In my teenage years I succeeded in pushing it to 9 p.m.

But Daddy was a firm believer in the Franklinism: "Early to bed, early to rise, makes a man healthy, wealthy and wise." Daddy was always in bed no later than 9 p.m.; he saw no reason why his progeny should be up later. Still, I yearned to "stay up like the big kids do."

I got my chance one New Year's Eve. My folks were going out, a rare occasion for them in those days. Grandma was staying with us three kids. I don't know what possessed Daddy to say it, but when Grandma asked what time we should be in bed, he replied, "I guess they can stay up 'til we get home."

I knew I had arrived! Mama and Daddy wouldn't be home until they had Auld Lang Syned in the New Year and that would be well after midnight.

Of course, there was no television to watch, and it seemed there was nothing very exciting on the Philco radio—what with the holiday and everything. Little sister Donna was the first to succumb, a little after 9 p.m. Dennis was next, about an hour later. I was alone in my bleary-eyed effort to "stay up like the big kids do."

I don't remember much else. Grandma either was touched by my valiant battle against sleep or was just too weary to put me in bed herself. At any rate, the next thing I knew there were muffled, dreamy voices, and I was hoisted in Daddy's powerful arms and carried off to the bedroom. As he tucked me in, I'm sure I protested, "But I want to stay up like the big kids do!"

Many years have gone by since. Daddy's way stuck with me, and I'm the most content today when I'm "early to bed, early to rise." Janice and I raised our own three children with a 9 p.m. bedtime—a bit old-fashioned, I'm sure, for the television generation. I heard many youthful complaints that were the equivalent of "I want to stay up like the big kids do," but they were to no avail. I just smiled inwardly, remembering my own futile attempt on that New Year's Eve back in the Good Old Days.

—*Ken Tate*

Facing page: *Good Old Days* magazine cover, January 1995, House of White Birches nostalgia archives
Home for Christmas by Lee Stroncek, courtesy of Wild Wings, Lake City, MN 55041

A Tap on His Shoulder

By Marie Grant

I t was 1933—a bitter-cold February morning. My brother was starting out on another day of job hunting. Mother followed him to the front door with needle and thread in hand. "Wait a minute, Harry," she said. "Let me try to fix that frayed cuff on your coat." She did the best she could with the cuff, kissed him, and told him she would pray.

"Don't waste your time." Harry slammed the door with such force the house shook.

My mother came into the kitchen where I was having breakfast. "Marie," she asked, "let's pray together for Harry." We knelt right there on the cold kitchen floor, mother and daughter, each praying in her own way for a son and brother.

I knew my mother's prayer was not only that Harry would find work, but that he would regain his faith in God. Harry had recently told me he no longer believed in God.

Seek, and you shall find; knock, and it shall be opened unto you.

I knew my brother was wrong, but I couldn't help feeling sorry for him. In addition, Harry was madly in love with Joan Connors, his childhood sweetheart, but he could not marry her until he found work. With each passing day, this seemed more and more like an impossible dream.

Within the past month, my father's salary had been cut and I had been put on part-time at the bookstore where I worked. As the Great Depression intensified, Harry became more hostile and bitter.

Maybe the job hunting went better today, I thought when I heard Harry whistling as he came up the front walk. I knew I was right at the dinner table that night. Between praises for Mother's cooking, Harry told us about his day.

"Remember, Dad," Harry started his story, "I told you I was determined to be first in line this morning for the job I saw advertised? Well, as early as I got there, there was a fellow before me—and he was hired."

"I'm sorry, son." My father looked pained.

"No, no, Dad," Harry said, "wait until you hear the rest of the story. I thought as long as I had paid my fare to go to the city, I would do the rounds of the employment agencies. No luck, of course."

"You should have come right home," Mother said. "It was too cold a day for you to be walking around the city."

"It was cold," Harry admitted. "And when I couldn't take it any longer, I decided to head for home. Now, here's the odd part." Harry's voice lowered. "I was halfway down the subway stairs when I felt something."

"Something? What kind of something?" I asked him.

"If you laugh, Sis, I won't tell the rest of the story," Harry threatened.

"She won't laugh. Go on, son," Mother said.

"I felt … I felt a tap on my shoulder." Harry's speech quickened. "So I turned around, but no one was there."

"What do you think it was?" I felt chilled.

"I don't know." Harry spoke slowly. "And I know you won't believe this—I heard a voice."

"A voice!" I couldn't contain myself.

"What did you hear, son?" Mother put her hand on my arm to silence me.

"I heard the words 'Go back.' Somehow, I knew what I was supposed to do—go back to the place where I had been too late this morning. That's exactly what I did."

"How could you do that," I asked, "after the man told you the job had been taken? Weren't you embarrassed?"

"That's the odd part of it," Harry said. "I wasn't. In fact, I felt very at ease

with the young man who was doing the hiring. He even told me to call him by his first name, Bernie."

"How about the job?" Dad asked.

"I got it." Harry stated happily.

"What about the other fellow," Mother worried.

"Wait 'til you hear this." Harry reached for another helping of potatoes. "The fellow who had been hired called Bernie and said he had changed his mind—he didn't want the job."

"Changed his mind!" Dad was in shock. "With thousands of people out of work, a guy calls and says he doesn't want the job! Why?"

"It seems," Harry explained, "his future father-in-law is chairman of the board of a large company and offered his future son-in-law a place in the firm."

"There's an old saying," Dad said, "that goes something like this: 'It's not *what* you know, but *who* you know.'"

"There's another old saying: 'Seek, and you shall find; knock, and it shall be opened unto you.'"

"Have you told Joan?" I wanted to know.

"Not yet," Harry answered. "I'm going to call her right after dinner. The best part of it all is, I'm going to be working for Bernie, and I like him very much. I feel as though we could become friends. He said he had been calling himself all kinds of a fool for not taking my name and phone number. He kept asking me over and over again what had made me come back. He seemed to feel as much at ease with me as I did with him."

"What did you tell Bernie when he asked you what made you come back?" Mother wanted to know.

Harry smiled at her. "I told him someone must have been praying for me."

Mother looked radiant. I knew her joy was not only because Harry had gotten a job. Harry was right. He and Bernie did become friends—such good friends that Harry invited Bernie to our house to meet Mother, Dad and his kid sister, Marie. Bernie and I fell in love. We married after a four-year courtship and will celebrate our 53rd wedding anniversary on Feb. 7, 1990. ❖

—*Originally published in February 1990.*

THE MAGAZINE THAT REMEMBERS THE BEST

GOOD ❖ OLD ❖ DAYS

JULY 1991

The Secret of the Old
Fishing Hole

Celebrating the Fourth in
Dynamite Style

John Slobodnik

FEATURING STORIES ❖ PHOTOS ❖ ILLUSTRATIONS
of the Happy Days Gone By

The Secret Fishing Hole

By Peter Hardwick

I admit it—my fishing skills were awful. My father joked that I would be better off staying home, claiming I left with more bait than I returned with fish. And whenever I *did* bring anything home, it was invariably a 3-inch pollock, the most common fish around our coast. By rights, these toddlers should have been thrown back, which is what I did when anyone was watching; but if I thought nobody was paying any attention, I'd glance around to make sure I was unobserved, then slip the unfortunate creature into my haversack. Mom would fillet and fry my "catch," toasting a slice of bread to spread it on. By passing it off as a snack rather than a meal, she helped save my dignity, because by the time my pollock had cooked down, there was barely enough left to cover the center of a saucer, let alone a plate.

"We've got a natural fisherman here," Dad said one Saturday.

What made my fishing appear even worse was my younger brother, Paul, who had only recently developed an interest in fishing, but had hit the luckiest streak I'd ever heard of! Rarely did he return without a catch. Most often, he stepped through the door carrying either a full-grown mackerel or a gray mullet. Once he held aloft a large, highly cherished bass.

"We've got a natural fisherman here," Dad said one Saturday, patting my brother's shoulder. "There's always a fish supper when Paul's out with his rod and reel."

Paul sat at the kitchen table one day with his quiet, wily smile, telling us how he had discovered the best place to fish.

"Why don't you take Peter with you this afternoon?" Mom said.

Paul looked at me, considering Mom's suggestion. "I could, I suppose," he finally said. "All right with you, Peter?"

I fetched our rods from the spare closet, pulled on my boots, and picked up my haversack that was always packed and ready. Paul collected his old weathered pack passed down by a neighbor, and off we went.

It's strange, I thought, as we headed toward the coast. *This is only the second time we have fished together.* The first time had been a complete washout. We had fished a small, muddy stream during a weekend visit to our grandparents. For over three hours, we stood on the banks, dangling our rods in the murky waters, waiting for a bite that never came. This afternoon promised more success.

"I'll try for a mullet," I said optimistically. Paul smiled. "We'll have to see what's biting."

He was taking a long way to the pier, the town's most popular fishing spot. I didn't think much about it until he turned left off Quay Road.

"Where are we going?" I asked.

"Chain Beach. That's where I get all my fish."

So he is going to try for mullet, I thought as we walked down Seaside Rise toward Chain Beach, a cove well known for its mullet—if you could catch them, that is. There were also bass farther out. A promenade made ideal fishing at high tide and steps led to the beach for fishing off the rocks at low tide. But steep cliffs on either side left the beach shaded for most of the day, so Chain Beach was rarely used.

"We shouldn't have much competition," I said. "Any hungry fish will be ours."

"That's right," said Paul as we walked onto the promenade. The tide was high and reaching toward the top step. We were the only ones there. I baited my hook and cast out. Paul was taking his time picking a worm and baiting up.

"Got a favorite worm?" I kidded him.

"I don't like to use my biggest worms early on," he replied. "I save them for when the fish are biting."

I couldn't argue with Paul's reasoning, nor his success rate. I just smiled. My younger brother, less than a year into his first fishing season, was already giving me tips. He cast out, reaching about the same distance as my line. I expected better after the reputation Paul had built, but he seemed content.

Soon we were sitting on the wall, our feet dangling above the water, keeping a loose grip on our rods. A couple of people wandered by in the first hour. They asked how we were doing, then left after hearing we hadn't caught anything.

Paul hadn't had a bite and wasn't bringing me much luck either. I was beginning to wish we had gone to the pier instead. At least we'd be among the usual crowd of school chums and older, experienced fishermen. I was about to suggest that we try the pier when my line jerked taut. "Here's my mullet!" I shouted, clutching my rod and swinging my legs over the wall so I could stand upright while reeling in my line.

"More like a pollock," said Paul, leaning over the wall, reminding me of my previous catches. Paul's instincts were more accurate than my wishful thinking, and soon I was in the semi-familiar position of kneeling beside my rod and unhooking a 3- to 4-inch pollock.

"I always throw those back," said Paul.

"So do I," I replied, glancing at him to make sure he was serious.

Even so, catching such a small fish still cheered our spirits. Within a minute we were back on the wall, rods gripped firmly, telling each other our next catch would be a fully grown mullet.

Now we looked forward to another passerby asking how we were doing, because although we still had nothing to show for over an hour's fishing, there was a fisherman's pride in being able to say we had thrown something back.

Paul and I began debating which we would see first, another bite or another visitor. Still flushed with renewed optimism, I insisted it would be my mullet next. Paul laughed, looking over his shoulder, saying that we would have a busload of visitors before I caught anything larger than the pollock I had just thrown back.

Although we didn't see any busloads, Paul did win the discussion when one of his classmates came along. It was John Harris, whose father's fish market we had passed on the way.

"How you doing?" he asked.

By now my imagination had swollen the pollock to a 6-inch fish that had put up an enormous struggle before being landed.

"Good going," said John. "I once threw back a 10-foot conger eel." I was wrestling with a suitable response when Mr. Harris' trawler pulled alongside the steps. John walked over to help his father unload the catch. Mr. Harris stood on the deck, greeting his son and waving to Paul and me.

"Caught anything, Paul?"

"Not yet, Mr. Harris."

"Try this!" He picked up a big mackerel and threw it our way. "Your brother want one too?"

Before I could answer, another mackerel flew toward us. I looked at Paul, who could barely suppress a smile. Already he was reeling in his line, preparing to pack up. "I told you this was the best place to fish," he said, snapping the lid on his tackle box. "We'll tell Mom the mullet weren't biting today." ❖

—Originally published in July 1991.

The Cookie Jar Caper

By Fred Van Sice

The cookie jar was always filled with big, delicious, sugar and molasses cookies that never seemed to run out—which was fine with me. Grandma allowed me one of each at dinner, and that was the limit.

But going to bed at night, thinking of those wonderful cookies was more than I could stand, so I began to plot just how I could retrieve a few without my grandmother finding out. The one thing that stood in my way was that the glass jar's top was a little loose, and it rattled when opened.

When no one was around, I practiced taking the cover off and found that if I lifted it just a little, I could stick my finger along the rim. Then, by letting the cover back down on that finger, I could tip it back and–*Eureka!*—the cover would release without a sound. I was elated! There they were, all mine for the taking. I then realized that I would have to "fluff up" the remaining cookies so it didn't look as though any were missing. Thus followed many nights of delicious adventure.

As years went by, I prided myself on my ability to open and close that cookie jar without being detected. The fact that it was always filled helped maintain that feeling.

My preoccupation with the cookie jar gradually lessened. Then the war came along. I remember the day I left for the service, with Grandma's hug and a box of my favorite cookies pressed into my hand. Those cookies kept coming on a weekly basis, and the boys in the barracks soon taught me about sharing.

Upon discharge I returned home and spent many an hour with Grandma, remembering the days of my youth. One of those conversations included my nights with the cookie jar. As I told the story, thinking Grandma had no idea of my shenanigans, I was surprised to see a faint smile cross her face.

Then she laughed, "I knew about the 'cookie caper' from the very beginning." My first thought was *How could she possibly have known, when I was so clever as not to make any noise and to keep the jar looking as if no cookies had been taken?*

But Grandma went on to say that she knew I was snatching, so she kept the supply coming so that I would think I was getting away with it. I sat puzzled until she explained. "The caper might have worked if it weren't for the cookie crumbs in your bed." ❖

—Originally published in September 1991.

THE MAGAZINE THAT REMEMBERS THE BEST

GOOD ⬩ OLD ⬩ DAYS

SEPTEMBER 1991 *When the Old Nag Outpulled the Mighty Steed*

Remembering Schooltime Pranks of Yesteryear

THE DELICIOUS ROASTED

Charles Berger

FEATURING STORIES ❖ PHOTOS ❖ ILLUSTRATIONS *Of the Happy Days Gone By*

Pitching a Pout

By Ethel K. Davis

Excitement filled our house the day before Thanksgiving in 1935. Daddy came home from work and we all walked down to the grocery store for our dinner trimmings. Daddy talked to Mr. King, the owner, while my sister and I helped Mama shop. I saw a jar of peanut butter on the shelf and begged her to buy some. Shaking her head, Mama said I'd have to wait until she had more money.

What a pout I pitched as I wistfully looked at all the jars of peanut butter lined up. When Mama called I grudgingly followed her voice. Mr. King finished packing our groceries, Daddy hoisted the box onto his shoulder and we left. I dragged my feet all the way home, pouting every step because I couldn't have some peanut butter.

We helped put groceries away as Daddy commented on how lucky we were. He told Mama he had heard at work that the Cullens family was so "down and out" that they wouldn't be having a Thanksgiving.

Suddenly, Mama just stopped putting groceries away and marched out of the kitchen. Daddy followed her, asking what was wrong. Struggling into her threadbare coat, she said she had forgotten some things at the store.

But Daddy knew her, and he said he did not think our budget could afford another Thanksgiving dinner. I'll never forget the look on Mama's face as she pulled her hat down over her ears and announced that she could not sit down and swallow one bite of food knowing that her friends were going hungry. Quickly, Daddy helped us into our coats, and we ran after her.

Mr. King teased Mama as we duplicated our order until Mama explained. As he packed the groceries, he cut the prices so he could help out too. Daddy smiled proudly at Mama as he hoisted the box to his shoulder. New excitement rippled through my sister and me as we skipped ahead of them, singing *Over the River and Through the Woods* all the way home.

Our kitchen looked like Mama was going to feed an army! As she put the rest of our groceries away, she suggested that Daddy take the box of groceries to the Cullens. Mama thought it would be best to ring the bell and leave so they wouldn't be embarrassed. Excitedly we watched Daddy drive off in our '29 Chevy.

The next morning, good Thanksgiving smells drifted into the dining room where my sister and I were filling nut bowls for Mama.

Suddenly I remembered my peanut butter! I asked Mama why I couldn't have a jar of peanut butter but she could buy a box of food and give it away. Surprised at my outburst, Mama explained that it was not right for me to have peanut butter when I really didn't need it and deny our friends Thanksgiving. She said it would be sad to have the Cullens' children sit down without all the good things we would have. Snuggled in her arms, I realized that the peanut butter wasn't important.

Knowing how much I loved peanut butter, Mama said that if I would be a good girl until payday, she would somehow manage to get me a small jar. Happy with those thoughts, I slid off her lap and went back to filling nut bowls.

That lesson has stayed with me all through life. Every time I see peanut butter in the market, I still think of the Thanksgiving when Mama taught me its real meaning. ❖

—Originally published in November 1991.

Our Uninvited Guests

By Calvin E. Sturdivant

On a cold day in 1933, my older sister and I were standing near the window, peering out at the snow. As we watched the flakes fall silently on the panes, visions of snowball fights and snow-cream were the childish things we thought of. But just then, our young, eager eyes were attracted to a strange sight. Through the windblown snow, a group of people walked close together as if they were trying to keep warm.

The railroad track we lived by was the main road for pedestrians, and though we had seen countless people pass our house, we never saw six walking in so strange a manner as these travelers. We kept our eyes trained on them as they neared our house. Their clothing was dirty and untidy and not suited for the conditions. They wore nothing on their heads, and their faces were the color of beets. Lo and behold, we noticed they were heading for our house.

Astonished, we watched them amble through our yard. I shouted, "Daddy, some white people are coming to our house!" By this time they were on the porch. The man knocked on the door, and Daddy immediately opened it. With a trembling, hoarse voice, the stranger said, "Sir, would you allow me and my family to come in and get warm? And if you can spare some victuals, we'd be much obliged. We're very hungry."

Dad welcomed them. "Come on in!" he said. "Yes, ya'll sure can get warm, and I'll have my wife fix ya'll some food."

"I sho' thank you, sir," came the reply from the weatherworn drifter. Our guests were a husband, wife and four children, two girls and two boys.

Daddy had us children—there were four of us—give the weary intruders our chairs, which we did grudgingly. Latha, my eldest sister, and I, stole off to a far corner of the room and began a low-tone criticism of the wayfarers. "Why did these poor ol' pecker-woods come to our house?" we said. "They

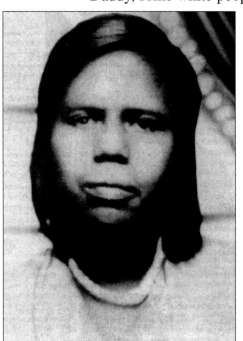

The author's mother in the 1930s.

know they don't even *like* colored people."

Meanwhile, Dad poked the fire and put a section of rock elm in the cast-iron heater to get the house warmer for our company. All the while, he chatted with the guests to make them feel comfortable. We could tell by their expressions that they were ill at ease.

He then turned to Mother. "Sugar," he asked, calling her by her pet name, "you think you can find some food for these folks?"

"Yes, I think so," she replied.

Off she went to the kitchen as the lady visitor offered a hearty "We sho' thank you." Soon the aroma of coffee filled the house.

My siblings and I scrutinized them with penetrating eyes. They were poorly dressed. Their clothes were tattered and torn, and their shoes were about worn out. Our young counterparts' noses were running; the boys' hair was long and needed trimming. We poked fun at them. We were young and foolish.

It took Mother 40 minutes to prepare the meal. "It's ready. Ya'll can come and eat now!" Mother announced as she emerged through the kitchen door. She had fixed grits, ham and eggs, biscuits, sorghum molasses syrup and coffee.

"Come on, let's go eat the food the missus cooked for us," the father said to his family.

They rushed into the kitchen. Daddy went in and said grace and our visitors ate voraciously. Mother packed the leftovers in a bag for them to take on their journey.

When they finished and had resumed their places around the wood stove, Daddy cut the boys' hair as he and the man talked about the state of the economy and the stock market crashing. (I suspect they knew as much about that then as I know about the budget deficit or the Gramm-Rudman Act now.)

The gentleman and his family had gone through dire times. His wife's sickness, a failed crop and other things beyond their control made life tough.

Suddenly our harsh, youthful cynicism ended and a metamorphosis took place: We were no longer little devils with horns, but guilty little souls with bleeding hearts.

Finally, our dejected guests prepared to leave. They had spent the better part of two hours at our home. The way they put on their cloaks and the grim looks on their faces told us more than they could ever say.

They left carrying the paper sack with them. My sister and I went to the window with lumps in our throats. There was nothing but silence in the room. The snow had slackened, but it was still cold. The Arkansas winter had come early that year. As we watched the impoverished wanderers vanish from sight, a pall of sadness fell over us.

Our family never forgot those folks, and we wondered what became of them. We also wondered why they stopped at our house; however, it was said that if you wanted to find food during those times, stop at a house where there are children. During the Depression years, my parents helped many others when hard times, hunger and destitution were the uninvited guests of so many. ❖

—Originally published in January 1992.

THE MAGAZINE THAT REMEMBERS THE BEST

GOOD · OLD · DAYS

Comfort Foods of the South JANUARY 1992 Back to the Old Skating Pond

FEATURING STORIES ❖ PHOTOS ❖ ILLUSTRATIONS Of the Happy Days Gone By

A Poor Boy's Gift

By Lisa Swan

You'll starve to death if you marry that boy!" my father warned me. "Your mother and I forbid you to see him again!" It was October 1940. I was 17 years old and desperately in love with Peter Swan. Peter lived in a foster home with six other boys nobody wanted.

On Oct. 17, Peter turned 18 and was allowed to leave the foster home. That morning he walked to my house to tell me he was leaving town. He was going to Joplin, Mo., where he'd heard about a job. He promised he would come back for me and we'd get married. But I knew that if he left without me, I'd never see him again.

"I'm coming with you!"

"You can't," he laughed. "I only have a few dollars and a long way to go. Besides, you aren't even wearing your shoes." I looked down. It was Indian summer, and I'd been walking around the yard barefooted.

Peter started walking down the road. Soon he'd be gone forever. I didn't dare go back into the house for my shoes or anything. If my parents knew what I was up to, they would stop me for sure. I ran down the road after Peter.

Not many brides elope barefooted, but I did. We caught a ride with a farmer and got as far as Neosho, Mo. Peter used some of his precious money to buy a pair of shoes for me, and we were married by a justice of the peace. Then we sent a letter to my parents, telling them.

Peter got a job at a bakery, and we rented a tiny room. It was heaven to me. December came, and we were looking forward to our first Christmas together. I had a long list of gifts I wanted to buy for Peter, but there was a fire in the bakery and it shut down for a month. There

would be no money for gifts. We might not even have enough money for food or rent.

We put all of our food on the kitchen table. We were carefully dividing it into piles for the coming days to plan our meals when there was a knock on the door. Some young men were collecting food for poor families for the holidays.

"Well, I'm broke, but this pretty girl loves me, so I'm not poor," Peter told them. Then he gave them half of our food. "I don't want any kids to go hungry at Christmas!"

I looked at the small pile of food that remained. It wouldn't feed us for the rest of the week. No gifts, no money and now no food—but I had never felt so loved.

Two days before Christmas, the men who had been collecting food were back—but this time they carried groceries to our doorstep!

"We gathered up food for the poorest family in the neighborhood, and we decided it was you," one of the men said, smiling. "Here's a card from the church. Merry Christmas." Five boxes of groceries and a turkey filled our kitchen. Inside the card was a $20 bill with an invitation to the Christmas Eve potluck dinner at the church.

"When we gave food to help the poor, I sure didn't know it was for us!" Peter said. "When I'm with you, I feel like the richest man in the world."

I've been married to that wonderful man for 50 years, and in spite of my parents' warnings, I never starved. We had three children, and every Christmas, Peter always gave away half of the food in our house to the poor. "For luck," he'd say. Well, I guess it works, because I've always felt like the luckiest woman in the world! ❖

—Originally published in February 1992.

Mama! Mama! Daddy's Dead!

By Dina L. Hunter

The year was 1943, and I was 5 years old. We lived near Loma Rica, Calif., on a small ranch. Our main crop was olives, but we had a few cows that grazed on the grass beneath the olive trees. Daddy was my hero. I followed him everywhere. Things happened when Daddy was around, and I didn't want to miss out.

One particular autumn day stands out vividly in my memory. Daddy and I walked through the orchard, checking the olives. The trees were loaded with big, glossy, purple olives. They looked so good hanging all along the thin, wiry branches.

"Can I have some olives, Daddy? Can I? Huh? Can I?" I begged. Daddy picked a few and handed them to me.

"What are you going to do with them?" he asked.

"Play with them," I said, and I put them in my pocket. I knew better than to eat them. I'd tried that last year, and they were awful. They were bitter. But I loved the smooth, satiny feel of them and carried them in my pocket, touching them often.

In a way, Blacky's eyes and Daddy's looked alike. That scared me.

We entered the barn, and Daddy took a coil of rope from the wall. "Now you stay here, out of the way," he said as he re-coiled the rope. "I'm going to lasso that cow out there," he said, pointing to old Blacky, "and we'll take her to the auction."

"Okay," I said, climbing up on the gate so I could see.

Daddy threw the lasso at Blacky. As the rope whizzed toward her, she shook her head and ran off. Daddy followed and tried again. But Blacky ran, and the lasso landed on her back and slid to the ground.

"Hold still, dang it!" Daddy said as he coiled the rope. He walked slowly toward Blacky, calling softly, "Come boss, come boss."

He missed again. "Hold still, you cantankerous old cow!" he yelled.

Daddy was really getting mad now. I could tell because his neck was getting red, and his eyes were looking kind of wild.

You didn't want to bother him when he looked like that, so I stayed as quiet as I could, cringing each time he threw the rope and missed. Each time he yelled a little louder at Blacky, and each time poor old Blacky kicked up her heels and ran.

You could tell she was upset, too. Her neck wasn't red, but her eyes sure were rolling and wild-looking.

In a way, her eyes and Daddy's looked alike. That scared me.

Finally, the lasso settled over Blacky's head. She let out a loud *Mooooo!* and bolted, jerking Daddy off his feet. Daddy flew through the air, then landed on his stomach, his head hitting the trunk of an olive tree. He lay still and the cow ran off, the rope trailing limply behind her.

I stood there, clinging to the gate. What was I to do? Daddy had said I should stay in the barn, and it just wasn't safe to cross him when he was mad. And he was definitely mad. But now he was hurt.

Finally, I tiptoed close to him and bent down to see his face. His eyes were closed, and he was still and pale. He looked dead.

"Mama! Mama! Daddy's dead!" I screamed as I flew through the orchard and across the road to the house.

"What!" Mama said. Now *her* eyes were wild looking and her face white.

"Don't you die, too, Mama!" I sobbed.

Mama started shaking me and screaming, "Where is he? Where is he? Come on, show me!" She grabbed my hand, and we ran back through the orchard, both of us crying.

We could see Daddy crawling on hands and knees under the olive tree, shaking his head. He looked up at us, grinning foolishly, a smear of blood on his forehead.

"You stupid idiot!" Mama yelled. "What do you think you're doing? I thought you were dead! You're an olive grower, not a cowboy! When are you going to learn and stop lassoing cows?"

I stared at my mother in amazement. She was crying and screaming at Daddy because he wasn't dead after all. And she was throwing olives at him. She kept stripping them off those little whiplike branches and throwing them at him.

Daddy just kept looking up at her and grinning. Finally, he collapsed in a heap and roared with laughter.

Mama threw a final handful of olives, grabbed my hand and marched to the house.

Awhile later, I watched Daddy walk toward the house, still grinning. As he came through the front door, trying to hide his grin, Mama threw down the broom. "Darn you!" she said. "You scared me to death!" Then she ran to him.

He grabbed her in a big bear hug and, still grinning at me over the top of her head, said, "I guess we won't be going to the auction today." ❖

—*Originally published in February 1994.*

THE MAGAZINE THAT REMEMBERS THE BEST

GOOD ❖ OLD ❖ DAYS

FEBRUARY 1994

Little Outhouse On the Prairie

Valentine's Day Circa 1934

GOOD ❖ OLD ❖ DAYS

John Slobodnik

FEATURING STORIES ❖ PHOTOS ❖ ILLUSTRATIONS
Of the Happy Days Gone By

The Short Straw

By Russell Ford

Living away from home at Tuscaloosa, Ala., I was a self-sufficient 19-year-old. I had saved a portion of my $105-a-month salary and had recently paid cash for a 1937 Dodge Town Sedan. The auto attracted a number of fellows who, desiring Saturday evening transportation, suggested they could introduce me to the most intelligent, cutest, most gorgeous young lady in Tuscaloosa County.

One Wednesday I told Frank, an old man of 35 years, "I'm not going home this weekend. Get me a date with that girl."

Saturday evening, Oct. 19, 1940, I picked up Frank and his wife. I was annoyed when Frank directed me to pick up another old couple. Rather shy, I had been on only two dates, and was bewildered by the thought of a girl I had never seen before being shoved against me. Would I be able to reach for the gearshift?

The girl was not home. A very apologetic mother explained her daughter had gone to Birmingham to see the Alabama-Tennessee football game. The girl was expected home momentarily.

I sat, fidgety, listening to trivial chitchat that was meaningless to me. Time dragged. After about 30 minutes, seeing that I was agitated, the girl's mother suggested that maybe she could find me a date. She disappeared out the back door.

She returned and said, "Come with me. Several girls said to bring you around."

My quaking knees made walking difficult, but I followed the woman down an avenue and around a corner to a house on the next street. Stumbling up steps onto a porch, I heard the *plink-plank* of a piano and a female chorus singing, "We kissed in a field of white, and stars fell on Alabama last night."

The author and his wife on their wedding day in 1941.

I wanted to cut and run. Never in my 19 years had I kissed a girl. The door opened and, upon entering the living room, I felt six pairs of piercing female eyes giving me the once-over.

"Who wants to go with him?" one girl asked.

"Let's draw straws," another suggested.

"I'll get the broom," a third volunteered. In a festive mood, the girls gathered around me as I plucked six straws. They lined up, but before one straw was drawn, the back door slammed.

"Must be Sybil," one girl remarked.

"Maybe she'd like to draw."

"I'll go ask."

A vivacious blonde entered the room and said, "He looks harmless. I'll play."

I blushed and nervously prepared a seventh straw. Seeing the blonde take her place at the end of the line, I prepared an eighth straw, visibly shorter than the other seven. I palmed the short straw.

My knees banged and my hands shook when Sybil stood waiting to draw the last straw. I managed to draw down the long straw and advance the short straw from my palm. She reached and our fingers touched. I felt electricity.

Because of my age, we had to secure her father's permission to marry. He said, "Son, if she'll have you, you better grab her." The ceremony took place on Feb. 8, 1941.

Soon after our marriage, it became apparent that I could not afford to keep the Dodge *and* my bride. I chose to get rid of the automobile.

At times, I must admit, I have wondered: *Did I make the right choice?* But I know I did. The Dodge became scrap metal many years ago. My Sybil, on the other hand, has been purring along with hardly a grumble for 53 short years. ❖

—Originally published in February 1994.

Daddy, Make Hazel Stop!

By Hazel Humphers

Hazel, do you remember the three of us sleeping in the same bed?" Oma asked. My two older sisters and I had gotten together for lunch. That remark started a nostalgic recall of our childhood days.

"Yes, I think I do. Wasn't that right after Mama died, and Daddy moved us to Grandpa's farm? I was only 5 years old. That house had two bedrooms with one bed in each room."

"I remember you used to sleep in the middle, with your knees straight up in the air, Hazel," Rubye joined in.

Her remark brought a flood of old experiences to my mind. Oma and Rubye had made me sleep in the middle because I was the youngest. I didn't like it one bit. They didn't like me setting my knees up because—they said—when I went to sleep, my legs fell over onto them.

"I'm not touching you!" I'd reply, but I wouldn't straighten my legs out. Then one of them would call out to Daddy who slept in the other bedroom.

"Daddy, make Hazel straighten out her legs."

"Hazel, straighten out your legs," Daddy said.

One night, Oma's girlfriend spent the night with us. Four in a bed was too much for me. I got up and lay down on the floor. Oma called out, "Daddy, make Hazel get back in bed."

"Hazel, get back into bed," Daddy said.

Every night, I said the prayer Mama had taught me—"Now I Lay Me Down to Sleep." Then I'd add, "God bless Daddy, God bless Oma, God bless Rubye, God bless Baldie (our dog), God bless Puss (our cat), God bless Button (our saddle horse), God bless the chickens, God bless the cows."

When I got to "God, bless Aunt Lora and …," Oma or Rubye would call out, "Daddy, make Hazel stop praying."

"Hazel, stop praying and go to sleep," came Daddy's quick reply.

Many years have gone by. My sisters and I love each other dearly. But sometimes, I wonder if I was earnestly talking to God, or if I just wanted to aggravate Oma and Rubye. ❖

—Originally published in September 1994.

THE MAGAZINE THAT REMEMBERS THE BEST

GOOD ∙ OLD ∙ DAYS

September 1994

A Surprise at
The Box Supper

Yesterday's Toys
My Magic Grandma

FREE AIR

FEATURING STORIES ❖ PHOTOS ❖ ILLUSTRATIONS
Of the Happy Days Gone By

Haircut Capers

By Edna Bright

B e good," Mother called as she waved goodbye to us. She walked up the street to Nellie's Home Beauty Shop for a haircut. Nena was 9 and I was 7. Mother trusted us to take care of the house the hour-and-a-half she would be gone. We sat on the porch swing for a while, then went inside for cookies. Back on the porch, we watched the cars go by.

Soon boredom set in, and Nena said, "Let me give you a haircut. I know how, for I've watched Daddy give Bill and Chet haircuts lots of times. I'll get Daddy's barber tools." She flitted inside.

I agreed to the haircut, but I said, "OK, you do mine, and then I'll do yours." We set up shop on the porch.

I loved Nena and looked up to her as my big sister who knew everything. When she started cutting my orange-red hair, I didn't resist, even when handfuls of hair fell to the floor. I didn't worry because I knew Nena had watched Daddy cut hair many times.

"I'm not about to let you use scissors on my curls," Nena protested.

Giggles erupted from Nena as she worked on one side and then the other. "What's funny?" I asked.

Nena just kept cutting and said, "Your hair's looking good."

Finally, with a flurry, she whipped the barber cloth off my shoulders and told me to go look in the mirror.

I was shocked. I was completely shorn, with large gaps here and there. I was ruined! But I kept my cool. I slicked my hair down with my hand and went back to the porch where Nena was still snickering.

"OK, it's your turn," I said as I shook the cloth and made ready to put it on her.

But Nena stepped back. "You can't cut hair," she protested. "I'm not about to let you use scissors on my curls."

"You promised," I said. "Now come on, get in the chair."

Nena was not only two years older; she was also bigger and stronger. A fight ensued. We were still going great when Mother came home.

Nena ran through the house and on out into the back yard. I stood forlornly on the porch.

Mother gasped when she saw my hair. But then she hugged me and said, "Now aren't you a pretty thing!"

I told her what had happened, and as she went inside, she called, "Nena, come here. I've something to show you."

Thinking Mother had brought her something, Nena bounced back into the house.

"Look, Nena, what a nice haircut I got," Mother said, twirling around for Nena to see. "Jan's is cut nice and short, too," Mother continued. "Don't you want to be in style like we are?"

Nena fidgeted, knowing full well what Mother meant. "No!" she blurted out. "I like mine like it is! I don't want a haircut!"

Mother went on out to the porch with me close behind. Nena hung back and started crying. Mother got the chair situated and looked at Nena as she pointed to it. Mother picked up the scissors and comb and handed them to me.

By now Nena was crying hard. I raised the comb and scissors and started to cut, but I stopped in midair. I wanted to cut Nena's hair, but my trembling hands wouldn't let me. I handed the scissors and comb to Mother and ran into the house.

Turning Nena to face her, Mother said, "You have hurt your little sister very much. Why did you do that?"

"I thought I could do it," Nena sobbed. "I've watched Daddy so many times, but when I got to cutting it, it wouldn't even up. I'm sorry it looks so terrible."

"The haircut is not the worst part," Mother said. "You've ruined Jan's trust in you. You know how much she loves you and looks up to you. How do you think she feels right now?"

"I'm sorry," Nena blubbered. "I'll go talk to her."

"No, not yet," Mother said. "Just sit there awhile and think about what you have done—not just to Jan's hair, for it will grow back, but think about betraying a loving trust. Jan may never trust you again."

Mother came inside and found me playing with the kitten on the kitchen floor. She pulled me onto her lap, and after a gentle rocking, she whispered, "It will grow back soon. Your beautiful red hair will come back prettier than ever. Just you wait and see."

Soon Nena joined us in the

kitchen, her eyes red and swollen. "Jan," she said to me, "you're the best sister in the world. I'd give anything if I hadn't ruined your hair. I wouldn't blame you if you cut off all of mine. Can you forgive me?"

I turned away, for I was still angry and hurt. Nena begged, and I hesitated. But when she hugged me, I melted.

"Yes, I'll forgive you, but I won't ever forget this haircut!" I declared. "I'm *never* going to a beauty shop when I get big!"

And the truth is, I *don't* enjoy going to the beauty shop. Could that traumatic haircut I had when I was 7 be the reason my hair is still red at 72—and why I'm still reluctant to let anybody style it? ❖

—Originally published in March 1996.

My Checkered Apron

By Dorothy Martin

I just want to talk a spell with you about the times we're living in. I guess I'm old-fashioned, but everything is going just a little too fast for me. All these fancy cars out there are going like crazy and running into each other. Now, back when I was growing up, we took things a lot slower, but we usually got where we were going. But now, everything is so modern and sophisticated, about all you need to do is just push a button. All these new inventions, though, can only do about one thing.

Now, you take a toaster. All it can do is make toast. A washing machine can only wash clothes. An iron can only iron, and so on.

I have something so simple, yet it can do more things than you can shake a stick at. That's my old red-checkered apron. It's just a piece of cloth, but it's like an old friend: always there when I need it.

Now, when my young sweetheart and I got married and started keeping house, we sure didn't have much except lots of love and determination. Our very first Christmas, he gave me a package all wrapped up so pretty, and when I opened it, there was this brand-new red-checkered apron. Oh, the things we have gone through together! Me and the apron, that is.

Me and my hubby had a little old rocky farm, and that red-checkered apron helped me in more ways than one. When I was cooking or baking, I didn't have any use for fancy pot holders. I just grabbed up my apron tail and got along just fine. And more than once, I've opened the

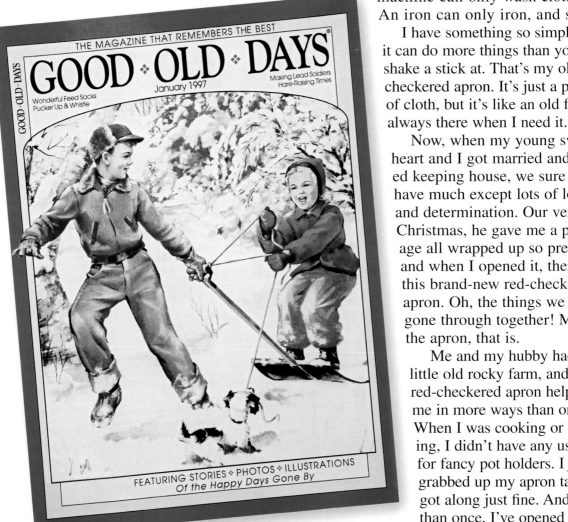

THE MAGAZINE THAT REMEMBERS THE BEST
GOOD · OLD · DAYS
January 1997
Wonderful Feed Sacks
Pucker Up & Whistle
Making Lead Soldiers
Hare-Raising Times

FEATURING STORIES ❖ PHOTOS ❖ ILLUSTRATIONS
Of the Happy Days Gone By

door and used it to fan the flies out. Back then we didn't have screen doors.

Airplanes were just getting started. When I'd hear one a-coming, I'd drop whatever I was doing and run out into the yard, waving that red-checkered apron for all I was worth. The plane wasn't too high, and the pilot would sometimes see me; I know, 'cause one time he tipped the wings a little as he went over to let me know he had seen me.

Then there were times the evenings would get pretty cool, and I'd just wrap that apron up around my arms like a shawl. Worked real good to keep the chill off. And I've carried many a corn cob in that apron to help kindle the fires.

And there was all my garden stuff. If I was caught without a basket, I'd gather that apron full of vegetables. And it was always handy if I found a hen nest. I've carried an awful lot of eggs in that apron.

And times when there were storm clouds a-coming, I'd gather those fluffy little chicks in my apron and take them to a safe place 'till the storm was over. And when I worked in the fields, that apron was the best ever to wipe sweat and to fan with the tail of it to help keep cool.

Then the babies came along. There is nothing in this world any sweeter than holding your baby, wrapped in that apron, warm and close to your heart. And the times while the baby was sitting on my lap, we would play peekaboo behind that apron—oh my, how we would laugh!

When all the bloody knees and bruises came along, it would come in handy to wipe the tears away. And that apron was an awful good hiding place for one of the shy ones when a stranger came along.

I have to smile when I remember my neighbor who lived across the road. Each wash day she would hang dainty lacy handkerchiefs on the line to dry. I saved myself a lot of work; I'd just say, "Come here, child," and use that apron tail for a hanky on their little noses. Worked mighty good, and was awful handy.

But there was one time when my apron got me into a mite of trouble. I was over in the pasture when I spotted this apple tree just loaded with big, beautiful apples. Now, I could already smell that hot apple pie I could fix for supper. So I gathered up that apron and filled it with some of those apples.

I was just starting back across the pasture when my better half hollered and said that something was behind me. Well, I looked around, and there was an old Jersey bull, a-pawing the ground and making the dirt fly. Now, you know, bulls for some crazy reason are not too fond of red. Well, he took in after me, and I took off a-running.

Now, this fence I had to get over was about 5 feet high, with four barbed wires at the top. My hubby said I took a flying leap, cleared that fence with plenty of room to spare, and never dropped an apple. 'Course, I know he was exaggerating, but my, he did love to tell that story! By the way, I remember the pie was awful good.

I can just see us waving those red-checkered aprons like banners.

You know, I was just thinking. I wouldn't be a bit surprised if, when all mothers go through those pearly gates, the Lord Himself will hand each one a brand-new red-checkered apron. Oh, I know there won't be any noses to wipe and certainly no tears to wipe away, 'cause the Lord's already done that. But I can just see us waving those red-checkered aprons like banners while we march around that throne, just a-praising God for all the good things He's done for us.

Well, I could go on and on, but I guess I've taken enough of your time. Just wanted you to know that the simplest things in life can sometimes bring the most pleasure. I just can't imagine anyone going through life without a red-checkered apron.

I don't wear it much anymore, 'cause it's getting pretty faded and worn. But it still hangs on a nail on my kitchen wall, a reminder of all the years we've spent together, good years as well as the bad. And somehow it brings comfort to my heart, just knowing we've been together so long, and we've grown old together.

Yes, that red-checkered apron has been a big part of my life. ❖

—Originally published in January 1997.

The Best Player the Yankees Never Had

By Ruth Carpenter

Once when I visited my brother, Jim, during his long illness, I handed him a dirty baseball. He took it in his bony hands and turned it over to touch the broken seams. Then he curled his fingers about the ball, ready to throw to first base, or perhaps home plate. He looked up at me, his eyes shining with tears he refused to shed.

"I didn't keep my promise, did I, Sis?" he asked.

I thought back to a cold March day when Jim and his best friend, Red, stayed after school to practice batting and fielding, hoping they could get positions on Emerson Elementary School's baseball team.

They were fifth-graders, while I was in sixth grade. All of us loved baseball, but Jim was determined to be a shortstop for the New York Yankees.

Mama had ordered me to come home right after school, and I fussed around the house, cleaning my room and helping with supper. I was just setting the table when Jim dragged his bat through the front door.

> *"I'm shortstop, and Red is first baseman. Just watch us win!"*

"How'd you do?" I asked.

"We spent most of the time chasing balls," he complained. "We'll never get on the team if we have to spend all our time running after balls."

He squinted up at me. "Why don't you stay after school tomorrow and get the balls for us?"

Mama agreed I could, and all afternoon, the boys took turns at batting and fielding. It seemed to me they weren't good fielders—I chased more of the battered balls than they did.

Batting didn't look too hard, and just before we went home, I persuaded Jim to let me try. He pitched a ball and I hit it—but not hard; it dribbled just a few inches in front of me. Red laughed, but Jim looked thoughtful.

"She hit it," he reminded Red. "Maybe she has a good eye. And I'll bet she'd get to first base. Nobody could field that ball fast enough to get her out. She can run fast."

For the next two weeks, I chased balls while they practiced. Sometimes they let me bat, but I never hit the ball again.

The coach scheduled tryouts for a Monday. Mama said I had no business staying for the tryouts, so I went home. But I met Jim at the front door when he came in, just in time for supper.

"How'd you do?" I demanded.

Jim whooped. "We both made the team! I'm shortstop and Red is first baseman. Just watch us win!"

The season ran through the rest of the school year and through the summer. The elementary schools played their games in the city park, and the Emerson team won every game they played. Jim starred at shortstop and also at bat.

In October of the new school year, Emerson met the champions of the elementary schools in a nearby town, and for that game, the teams played on Saturday night in the stadium our high school used. Jim had to be there early, so Mama, Daddy and I drove him out.

We watched as the boys practiced. They looked good to me. Finally the stadium lights came on and the visiting team took the field. They played well, but they couldn't get a ball past Jim—he seemed to be all over center field.

Daddy and I yelled ourselves hoarse, and even Mama clapped her white-gloved hands. It was just like a movie. Neither team could score. Then, in the last half of the last inning, Jim hit a home run. Our team went wild, pounding Jim so hard I wondered if he could stand up. Fans in the stands whistled and yelled "Jim!" at the tops of their lungs. The visitors looked stunned.

Jim was quiet on the way home, but Daddy and I made up for him. I could just see Daddy the next day, telling the men at the oil well how his son had won the game.

We finally got to bed, and I was just drifting off to sleep when Jim appeared beside me. He held out a dirty baseball. "This is the home-run ball," he whispered. "One of the guys found it for me, and I want you to have it. I tried to get the dirt off."

I sat up, took the gritty ball, and turned it over in my hands. Reverently, I touched the broken seam, sure that that was where Jim's bat had landed.

"I couldn't have made the team if you hadn't helped," he said. "And I promise someday I'll replace that ball with the first home-run ball I hit when I'm a shortstop for the Yankees."

Through high school, Jim was star shortstop for the school teams. Sometimes when he hit a home run, he would look up at me in the stands, raising his clasped hands over his head in salute.

But in December before the spring he dreamed of breaching the Yankee training camp, World War II erupted, shattering dreams. Jim spent three years on a Pacific island instead of playing shortstop for the Yankees.

More than 50 years later, I watched him touch the ball with the same reverence I felt the night he had given it to me.

"You kept a promise to your country," I told him. "That took precedence."

He curled his fingers around the ball. "Still a Yankee fan?" he asked, not looking at me.

"Always a Yankee fan," I promised faithfully. He looked up, smiling, and tossed me the ball. ❖

—Originally published in March 1997.

GOOD ❖ OLD ❖ DAYS®

GOOD ❖ OLD ❖ DAYS

City Santa
Unforgettable Christmas

December 1997

Mama's New Red Coat
Country School Christmas

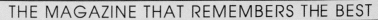

FEATURING STORIES ❖ PHOTOS ❖ ILLUSTRATIONS
Of the Happy Days Gone By

Mama's New Red Coat

By Ronald J. DeSantis

Who would ever think that an 85-year-old woman would keep buried in her heart a secret desire she had held since she was 5 years old? Certainly I wouldn't, and I'm her 45-year-old son. I found out by accident last fall when she came over for Thanksgiving dinner. I took Mom's coat. It was old, dull brown wool, with a dark brown velvet collar, threadbare in places. Four brown buttons—two of them mismatched—kept the front closed.

I asked when she was going to get a new coat, and I told her I would take her for a new one in the coming week. She refused and told me she was not wasting money on a new coat, for only God knew how much longer she would need it. I told her I was going to pay for it, but she refused. I said that $100 for her a new coat would not matter that much. Well, I said the wrong thing.

Since she had been a child, she had always wanted a red coat.

"One hundred dollars for a new coat?" she yelled. "Are you crazy?"

There was no arguing with Mother, especially over money. My wife, Ruth, suggested that we make it a Christmas present; then she couldn't refuse.

"Good idea," I answered. *How do wives always have the right solution?* I wondered. I broke the news to Mother and told her that we were not going to take no for an answer. After all, she couldn't refuse a gift.

"NO!" she said. After several hours of negotiations, she finally agreed. But, "It can't cost anywhere near $100," she said.

Ruth said she would take Mother for her new coat, but I said, "It's a mother-son thing." Big mistake.

I picked her up on Tuesday morning. First we went out for breakfast, our usual Tuesday-morning ritual. That's when she told me her secret. Since she had been a child, she had wanted a red coat. When she was 5 years old and living in Bradford, Mass., the girl down the street from them, whose father was a lawyer, had gotten a new red coat for winter.

Mother lived on a farm with her grandparents. There wasn't a lot of money, so anything other than a basic wool coat was not in her future. Coats then were warm and practical, but far from fashion statements. The only colors outside the finer stores in Boston were basic brown and basic black.

Facing page: *Good Old Days* magazine cover, December 1997, House of White Birches nostalgia archives
A Christmas Wish by Lee Stroncek, courtesy of Wild Wings, Lake City, MN 55041

Mother never knew her father; she was told he left her and her mother. She found out years later that it had been her mother who had left *him.* My grandmother worked in Haverhill in a shoe shop 12 hours a day, six days a week. She couldn't properly watch my mother, so it was off to the farm in Bradford with her Gran and Grandfather. My grandmother visited Mother on Sundays and holidays.

On the day in question, Grandfather and my mother had been delivering milk to the little girl's family. That's when my mother first saw and fell in love with the red coat. Though she never mentioned her secret wish to anyone, she would aspire to that red coat all her life. When she finally had a red coat, she would know she had made it.

Mother quit high school in her sophomore year to follow her mother's footsteps into the shops of Haverhill. Money was scarce, and the family needed her help.

One Saturday night, Mother went to a dance in Haverhill with her cousins. There she met a young man from a neighboring big city. My father was very handsome. At the time, he was an amateur boxer with the ring name "Kid Bobo." It was love at first sight.

They were married by a justice of the peace a short time later and moved in with his mother in Lawrence. Mom was 17 and Dad was 22 years old. As Dad was from a family of 12, there wasn't much room, but they made the best of it.

Dad had only a sixth-grade education, so all the jobs he held were menial ones. It was not much money, but honest work. My parents lived hand-to-mouth, week-to-week, their whole lives. Despite that, I never knew we were poor.

Enough of that, now—back to Mom.

Armed with several sale sheets from the local newspapers, we were off to find a new red coat for Mom. In the mall, the first women's store we came to had a red coat in the window. Easy—piece of cake, right?

Wrong!

Mom tried it on, but it cost $118. I told her that was all right. She said, "No." She liked the coat, but it was the wrong color red. The coat, she said, had to be red like the cheeks of her granddaughter, Kayla, in winter—not the red of a garden tomato.

Yeah, right, I thought.

I knew I was in for trouble. She was reading the price tag first.

Three stores and four red coats later, I was tired. The last coat I thought was perfect, but it cost $129. She pretended that it wasn't the money, but I knew it was more than Mom could allow me to spend without having nightmares.

I should have let Ruth do this.

"The coat is nice, son, but the color is a wrong red. It's a fire-truck red, not a Macintosh-apple-in-fall red."

I knew she had seen the price tag again.

Leaving the mall, we passed the last women's store. "Let's give it one more try, Mother," I suggested. This time I was ready. I stood right beside her and when she searched for the tag, I grabbed it and held my thumb over the numeral one of the $145 price.

"Look at this, Mom!" I shouted. "A sale, and it's a beautiful color of red!"

Mom saw only $45 on the tag and fell in love with the red coat. "Now *that's* a red coat, son," she said, pleased with herself. "That's the red I've been telling you about, the red in Kayla's cheeks, the red in the apples, but most important, the red in the August sunset the day we buried your father."

It looked like the same red of dozens of coats she had tried on throughout that long, long day.

The salesgirl tried to put it in a box, but Mom pulled the coat away from her. I made her go and look in the mirror again while I paid the bill so she wouldn't see the real price.

We walked out with Mom wearing her new red coat, strutting like a kid with new shoes.

The rest of the week was taken up with bringing Mom around to all her friends and relatives so she could show off the new red coat under the guise of having not seen them in a while.

It wasn't the only gift Mom got that Christmas, but I'll guarantee it's the only one she would remember.

Mother, exhausted from her lifelong labors, closed her eyes for the last time the next June. Friends and family members couldn't understand why we opted for a closed coffin. But when Mother met my dad, Kid Bobo, at the pearly gates, she was wearing her new red coat. ❖

—Originally published in December 1997.

Nothing to Fear

By Robert Hutchings

One of my fondest memories of growing up during the Depression is of listening to the radio. I liked *Jack Armstrong.* Mom's favorite program was the ongoing saga of *Ella Cinder,* while Dad liked to listen to the news and the farm reports. But the one program the entire family never missed was President Roosevelt's Fireside Chats. However, there was one rule: Before we were allowed to gather around the radio, we had to get our chores done.

I loved the chats and took great comfort in the president's words: "The only thing we have to fear is fear itself."

One evening, just as we were all comfortably around the radio, Dad asked me, "Bobby, did you lock up the corncrib?"

"Uh, yeah, Dad," I stammered, remembering full well that in my haphazard hurry to get my chores done, I had left it open.

Dad must have read my mind. "You better go check it just to make sure, son. We don't want the 'coons eating up all the corn."

I had gotten plenty of whippings from Mom; most of them I have forgotten. But Dad was an easygoing man with a sense of humor. I do not remember him ever whipping me, and he never yelled at me. When it came to discipline, Dad dished out his own brand of punishment.

Grumbling, I picked up the coal-oil lantern and headed back to the barn. The night was spooky and dark, with not a bit of moonlight. As I walked, the lantern swayed back and forth with each step, casting huge, grotesque shadows.

"Whoooooo, who-who!" A chill went up my spine when the eerie sound came from the nearby woods. *It's just an owl*, I told myself. But I picked up my pace.

As I stepped into the darkness of the barn, Tom, the big barn cat, let out a high-pitched *Meow!* and darted in front of me. His green eyes caught the lantern light as he glared at me from the corner. I hurried to the corncrib, latched the door and turned to head for the house.

My journey was almost over when something at the corner of the house caught my eye. It was huge and white. *Oh, it's only Bossy, the cow.* I breathed a sigh of relief and walked briskly.

"Oooooooo!" The thing moaned as it danced up and down. It wasn't Bossy. I froze in my tracks. I could see Mom through the window beyond me. She was sitting by the radio listening to those comforting words, "The only thing you have to fear is fear itself." Dad must have gone to bed, because I couldn't see him.

"Oooooooo!" The thing moaned as it danced up and down.

I tried to run, but my feet seemed to move in slow motion. The ghostly figure moved into my pathway. "Oooooohahaha!" it cried again, coming closer. I darted past, feeling a gust of air as it grabbed at me.

I dashed through the door and slammed it behind me. My heart was still pounding when I blew out the lantern and went to sit beside Mom.

"What's the matter with you, Bobby?" she asked. "You look as if you've seen a ghost."

I then heard a familiar "Hahahaha," and there was Dad, coming through the front door, a sheet draped across his arm.

"Just bringing in the laundry," he said, grinning. "But you know what? I think I saw a ghost out there. What do you think, Bobby? It sure is spooky out there. Did you see any ghosts?"

"No, Dad," I said as steadily as I could. "I never saw nothing but an old sheet flapping in the breeze." Then I added, "There's nothing to fear but fear itself."

When I went to bed that night, I made myself a solemn promise: *I will never forget to lock up the corncrib—and, furthermore, I will never tell another lie.* ❖

—Originally published in October 1997.

THE MAGAZINE THAT REMEMBERS THE BEST

GOOD ✦ OLD ✦ DAYS®

GOOD ✦ OLD ✦ DAYS

March 1998

FEATURING STORIES ✦ PHOTOS ✦ ILLUSTRATIONS
Of the Happy Days Gone By

How Tall Is a Tall Man?

By Frieda Guthrie

At the age of 84, my father came to my first husband's funeral—and he stayed for two years. During those two years, he and I became closer than we ever had been. We talked of many things. One interesting conversation was instigated by the question "Dad, what would you have changed in your life if you had had a chance?"

He thought for a while, then replied:

"Well, I don't rightly think of anything special, but I always wished I could have been taller.

"I was always the shortest one standing at the end of the front row in the school pictures.

"In a ballgame, I was always the last one chosen because I was shorter than the rest of the group, and I couldn't run as fast in a baseball game as the longer-legged ones. In a crowd, I never could see over the persons in front of me. I often wondered what they were looking at.

"So, I guess if I could have changed anything, it would have been my height.

"Maybe that's why I became a farmer. I enjoyed taking care of the farm animals. They never seemed to mind how small I was. They quieted down when I came around with their feed, or I cleaned the barn.

"I can't recall ever having had any mean animals to speak of. It must have been because I talked to them a lot. They seemed to like that."

The answer threw me a curve. My father was about 5 feet 6 inches tall, but since he was the idol of my childhood heart, he had never seemed short to me. I'm not too tall myself. I probably haven't gotten over 5 feet 4 inches in my prime.

But I could see that this was something he'd been brooding over for some time.

"In my estimation, you're the tallest man I've ever known."

After a few minutes, I said:

"Dad, you were always a tall man to me. When I was a wee little girl, you'd reach down to pick me up, and you were the nicest, tallest, big man I knew.

"You put up with holding me. You let me squirm around, cuddle, listen to your big watch tick, let me investigate your pockets, play with your hair and try to find a new way of parting it, collapse and go sound asleep in your arms, confident that I was safe and loved.

"You were always tall to me. I guess I always looked up to you because you were taller, and I loved you. Later, when we grew closer to the same height, it never occurred to me not to look up to you and your principles and the standards you lived by. In my estimation, you're the tallest man I've ever known."

Tears came to his eyes as he gently said, "That's just about the nicest thing anyone has ever said to me." ❖

—Originally published in March 1998.

Facing page: *Good Old Days* magazine cover, March 1998, House of White Birches nostalgia archives
Sugaring Off by Persis Clayton Weirs, courtesy of Wild Wings, Lake City, MN 55041

Warm as a Hug

By Happy Howard

our father needs a new coat," Grandma said, peering over her glasses at me as I blew on the frosty windows.

"I know, Grandma, but we don't have the money," I said, watching Daddy breaking the ice in the tank so the cattle could drink.

"I'd buy him one, but I know he wouldn't let me," Grandma said in her squeaky voice.

"Just don't tell him," I suggested.

"How? Gotta have measurements or it won't fit," Grandma said, shrugging her stooped shoulders.

"Yeah, that's a problem. Guess I'll have to figure out a way to fool him," I said, blowing some more frosty swirls on the window.

Grandma reached up and repinned her snow-white hair with crinkled, old hands. "You do that, child. But before he freezes."

As soon as the supper dishes were done and the table was cleared, we set it up for a card game. After a couple of hands, an idea struck me. I leaned over and asked Dad, "Do you think you're bigger than Mr. Salpas?"

Rubbing his bald head, Dad said, "Don't know. He's a fair-sized man. He's taller for sure, but I think I'm bigger around." He patted his barrel chest. "Why do you ask? It's your turn to bid."

"Just wonderin'," I said, trying to sound unconcerned. "I bid 400."

"Four hundred! I'm gonna set ya!"

He forgot about sizes as he plotted his game plan. His week's growth of beard couldn't hide his deep dimples as he chided me. "This time, daughter, you bit off more than you can chew!"

The next morning, I watched him shave as I always did, twisting my face this way and that as I mocked him. He daubed my nose with some shaving cream. It was our usual Sunday-morning routine. He didn't wear his glasses just so I could tell him the spots he missed.

While enjoying a big breakfast of pancakes, eggs, bacon, sausage and fried potatoes, I casually remarked as I looked Daddy up and down, "No, I don't think so."

Checking himself to make sure he hadn't spilled syrup on his shirt, he asked, "You don't think so what?"

"That he's bigger than you," I answered.

"Who?" Howard, my little brother asked.

"Helen's father," I said, in answer to his puzzled look. "Helen says her dad is bigger than Daddy." Before Howard could disclaim it, I gave him a kick under the table, which meant that he should be quiet.

Mom, somehow knowing that this was her cue, smiled at Grandma and said, "I would think measurements would settle it easily."

"Now why didn't *I* think of that?" I exclaimed. "You are so smart, Mom!"

"But it will wait until these dishes are done," Mom said. Covering her smile, Grandma almost choked as she tried to appear uninterested.

Later, standing on a chair with a measuring tape, I called out the inches as Mom wrote them down. Daddy puffed his chest up a little bigger to match his pride.

I was always Daddy's biggest cheerleader and his special little imp. If Mom didn't have my black hair in long locks, it was in pigtails. I would rather have had it cut off like a boy's, but Daddy preferred long hair on girls, so we compromised. It was kept long for Dad, but in pigtails for me, where it would stay out of my way.

In that day and age, little girls wore nothing except dresses. Except me. Dresses would never endure a day with me, so I got to wear some of my big brother's hand-me-down overalls—except for school, of course.

I lived so much in my bare feet that my soles were like rawhide. It seemed nothing could penetrate them. Rocks, glass, sandburs—nothing I stepped on even made a dent. I was a skinny tomboy, with dirty elbows and knees from all the places I explored, or just from tagging along behind Dad.

"Okay, that's the top. Mr. Salpas might be just a bit taller, but I'm sure he's not bigger," I said as I put the measurements into my arithmetic book. I knew Daddy was hoping his little girl wouldn't be disappointed.

A few days later, we could see Daddy waiting for us kids as we plowed through the fresh snow on our way home from school. He had taken Grandma into town to let her get some medicine and do some shopping she said needed doing. Mom stayed home and kept the fires a-going, and Daddy picked up some flour for her baking and some chicken feed.

Dad brushed the snow off us kids with the broom and sent us into the house a-huffing and puffing from the cold. Flinging off layer upon layer of clothing, we huddled up to the wood-burning cookstove. I checked out the big pot of bean soup and, unable to wait for supper, begged Mom for a slice of fresh home-made bread.

I knew that Daddy had been waiting for me to tell him who was bigger, he or Mr. Salpas, but his manly pride wouldn't let him ask. I guess he figured I would tell him sooner or later.

As we gobbled down Mom's great bread, Dad said with authority, "Soon as you finish, let's get the chores done."

As he reached for his patched, battered old coat hanging behind the kitchen door, Grandma said to Daddy, "Before you go out and do the chores, there's something in the pantry for you." She pointed for me to go get it. I was back in a flash with a big bag and handed it to Daddy. He was surprised as he pulled the new coat from the bag. He didn't know what to say.

"Put it on!" we all yelled together.

It fit perfectly. Looking at all our smiling faces, Daddy asked Grandma, "How in the world did you know what size to get?" But he knew the answer before the last word left his mouth. The silly smirk on my face told it all.

Snow crunching beneath our feet, we headed out to do our chores. "So who's bigger? Me or Mr. Salpas?" Dad asked teasingly.

"Don't know," I replied. "Helen would never measure her dad. She's afraid of him. If she even tried to touch him, he would probably knock her clear across the room. They don't talk, play cards or have fun together like we do. Even if he *was* bigger, it wouldn't matter. Bigger doesn't mean better. Next to my dad, he doesn't measure up!"

Chuckling, I gave him a sock to the arm and said, "You look real warm there, sir." I bounded off to the henhouse to gather the eggs.

A few days later, the sled showed up, leaning against the porch, its broken runner fixed. Someone also had taken the time to get inside my doll's head and fix the eyes so they would close again.

So I gave that someone a big hug. ❖

—Originally published in April 1998.

THE MAGAZINE THAT REMEMBERS THE BEST

GOOD ❖ OLD ❖ DAYS ®

GOOD ❖ OLD ❖ DAYS

Who Screamed?
Storm Trackers

June 1998

Unexpected Shivaree
A Walk With My Father

John Slobodnik

FEATURING STORIES ❖ PHOTOS ❖ ILLUSTRATIONS
Of the Happy Days Gone By

The Yellow Gingham Dress

By Frances Bell Pond

*H*ow else does one begin a love story other than "Once upon a time"? This is a true love story—a love story that was woven through the threads of a yellow gingham dress. and it does begin that way: Once upon a time, there was a little girl who lived with her parents on a farm in the country. She was a shy, plain-looking little girl, the youngest in a family with two brothers and a sister. I was that little girl.

Since there were no other children nearby, I spent much time alone, except for the constant companionship of a much-loved collie dog named Sport. Together we roamed the meadows and woods on the farm. I listened with fascination to the songs of the many different birds, and he chased squirrels. I was a child with a vivid imagination, so I never felt lonely. I could always call one of my make-believe friends to play with me or share some exciting secrets that I stored in my imaginative mind.

This is a love story woven through the threads of a yellow gingham dress.

I walked each day to a one-room school where I had a wonderful teacher. I learned so many interesting things about the world around me, and I also learned to read and to enjoy the beauty of poetry, which would one day lead to writing and publishing poems and short stories.

My parents were far from wealthy, so my clothes were always hand-me-downs or homemade by my mother. One dress above all others proved to be magical, for it became the star character in three important chapters of my life. It was made of yellow checked gingham, perfectly plain except for a wide, circular collar and gathered skirt—not at all like the satin, lace and chiffon usually associated with romance!

The years passed quickly. Public school days were over, and I was off to the city to take a commercial course at the Collegiate Institute. My first year was spent in the home of the school principal and his wife and small daughter.

Later, I rode a little steam train, which I boarded each morning at a small whistle-stop station. I would walk a mile to the station to catch the train at 6:50 a.m. and return in the evening at 7:10 p.m. to walk home.

Graduation from Collegiate came in June 1927, and I was now a young lady about to begin work as a stenographer in a bank in a town near my home.

The summer after I started to work, my mother died, leaving a terrible void in my life and, I am sure, in that of my father. The morning of her death, a university student named Harold who worked with my sister drove us to the farm. I had met him but once, but had watched each time he came into the bank, and I hoped that he might notice me.

Later that summer, one of his university chums spent a weekend with him, and he asked my sister if she and I might go on a date with them. It was a wonderful evening, spent on the beach at a camp near Normandale in southern Ontario. When it was over, I knew in my heart that I was in love. Young, impressionable, inexperienced—yes! But I knew how I felt!

I had been brought up by parents who didn't work on Sunday. But now things were different. My paternal grandmother, who was in her late 80s, had come to live with my dad on the farm, and although she provided company for him, many household chores were beyond her. So on the weekends, my sister and I would catch up on all the undone things.

One fateful Sunday afternoon I was busily engaged in doing the laundry. I had put on the little old yellow gingham dress from public school days and, barefoot, was in the back kitchen, hard at work. My grandmother appeared at the door and said there was a young man in the parlor who wanted to see me.

I was trapped! There was no way to get to my other clothes or my shoes without being seen, so I smiled bravely and entered the parlor—bare feet, gingham dress and all! We laughed together in spite of my embarrassment. He apologized for not having phoned, and he stayed for the rest of the afternoon and evening.

We dated regularly from then on, and the following year, on my birthday, he proposed to me.

Unbelievably, when he asked me to marry him, he said, "If you love me as much as I love you, I'd like to marry that little girl in the yellow gingham dress!"

I was ecstatic. I said, "Yes!" and we went to talk to my dad and grandmother. I knew that Dad liked Harold, and I knew that Grandma adored him, so it was easy.

We were married a year later, on June 27, 1930, in Simcoe, Ontario, but not before I heard those familiar words many times: "You're much too young; it won't last." But as we held hands to take our vows, I knew it would. We never really stopped holding hands. It became for us an unspoken way of saying how much we enjoyed sharing life together.

Our marriage was truly a happy one, lasting slightly over 65 years. The years brought us three loved and loving children who, in turn, married and brought still more love into our lives. Grandchildren and great-grandchildren endeared themselves to us and, as all our families lived nearby, we were never lonely. Wonderful friends, beautiful vacation trips,

"I'd like to marry that little girl in the yellow gingham dress!"

laughter and tears, work and worry, joy and happiness, a home and family we loved all became part of the 65 happy years together.

Then came two strokes, followed by total blindness for Harold. For me it was heartbreak, but as he had done for a lifetime, Harold met the challenge head-on. No complaints. Finally, hospitalized, he accepted the day-after-day boredom cheerfully, as I tried to fill those days with reading and news of family, friends and community.

I was grateful that he was pain-free and alert through it all, and will always feel that his complete trust in a loving heavenly Father gave him courage and strength to face the battle.

But age wouldn't be denied. Shortly after his 91st birthday, I noticed that he had become weaker and less talkative. Then, just the night before he died, when I tucked him in for a goodnight kiss, he smiled up at me and said in a whisper. "You know, Mum, I never stopped loving that little girl in the yellow gingham dress!"

At three very memorable times in my life, that dress was a star player. The first time was when that young university student came to see me; then, later, at my engagement; and finally, years later, when I lost Harold. He never forgot!

Perhaps that is why I can still see his face through the tears and can smile as I am writing this love story … the story that begins with "Once upon a time. …" ❖

—Originally published in June 1998.

Uncle Charlie's Wart

By June Edwards

On one of Uncle Charlie's visits, I was plagued and distressed by an unsightly wart on my right thumb. The wart seemed to develop almost overnight. It was always getting caught on something and bleeding, and besides, it was ugly, and I hated it. It didn't help any that my brother, Doog, had been teasing me about my "pet," asking me how many frogs I had played with to get such a big, old, ugly wart.

I guess Uncle Charlie wanted to take my part, for he told me, "Don't pay him no mind! That's money growin' out of you thar!"

I looked it over with a little less disgust and some interest.

"Money?"

"Yes, Ma'am! I buy warts, ye know."

"How can anybody buy a wart?" And I thought, *Why would anybody* want *to?*

"Well, I can! And I do. How much would ye take fer that little old wart, anyway? It's not quite as big as he said. A quarter?"

"A whole *quarter?*" We were talking about big money here! It sounded silly that anybody could or would even *want* to buy a wart. But a quarter was a quarter! I hesitated, but only for a second.

"Sure I will!" I answered. Why, I would have almost paid *him* a quarter just to take it—if I'd *had* a quarter.

"Tell ye what I'll do," he said. "I'll pay ye fer it today, but I don't want to take delivery yet. I'll let ye know when." And with that, he dug into his pocket and handed me a bright, shiny quarter. Then he looked the wart over, as if studying it for identifying markings before letting my hand drop. "Ye be sure and take good care of it till I come fer it now," he said. "Remember."

To say that I was tickled pink didn't even begin to describe it. I went to bed that night a really happy young'un, for sure.

I don't know how long it took, nor how many visits Uncle Charlie paid us before he decided to "take delivery" of "his" wart, but every time he came, he would ask to check it out, saying something like "I can see ye've been mindin' it real well, but I don't think I can take it with me today. I guess ye'll just have to keep it fer a spell yet."

There came a day, though, when Uncle Charlie paid a call, and rather than ask to see it, he said straight out, "I guess I'll take my wart today."

I glanced down, and to my utter surprise, I had somehow lost his wart! But instead of being upset, kind man that he was, he said, "Well, to tell ye the truth, I've kinda lost my yen for warts lately anyway. I was just gonna take it off yer hands, just in case ye'd got tired of mindin' it for me."

He had covered all his bases, even figuring a way to keep me from feeling duty-bound to give him back his quarter.

And probably a good thing, too, for thinking that wart would be available for delivery even if he waited 10 years, I had probably spent the quarter on our first shopping trip to town.

It was years before I understood that he had always surreptitiously checked to see if the wart had spontaneously disappeared (as I understand warts are prone to do) before he told me he wanted to check it out. Of course, he decided he wanted to take delivery only after he learned it was gone.

As my grandchildren came along and developed warts, I tried my prowess at wart-buying. But as far as I know, my magic powers never worked, and they may still be waiting for me to "demand delivery."

I'll bet it would have done Uncle Charlie's heart good to know that his kindness to a little girl was to stay on in *her* heart for over 70 years! Maybe he *did* know it. I hope he did! ❖

—Originally published in July 1999.

Watermelons And Outhouses

By Bill Connell

This amusing story comes to mind each year as summer approaches. It took place in 1941, when I was a young boy. I got to spend each summer at my grandpa's farm in Dover, N.J. Being a city boy, this was a big thrill for me. I could romp and play all summer with my two friends, Basil and Robbie. I had only a few chores to do; the rest of the day, I was free as a bird. Grandpa's farm was of a fair size and had all the usual farm items. He grew fruits and vegetables and sold them to folks in the area.

About a quarter-mile down the road was another farm. It belonged to the meanest, dirtiest-looking old farmer called Farmer Ferdinand. No one wanted to go near him. He had a wife, but no one ever saw her.

One evening, Basil, Robbie and I decided to sneak onto Farmer Ferdinand's property to borrow a watermelon. During this escapade, Farmer Ferdinand came out of the house. As we ran, we heard a couple of loud bangs. All of us caught some rock salt in our backsides.

My wonderful summer vacation turned into a nightmare.

When I arrived back at Grandpa and Nana's, I was in a lot of pain and shedding lots of tears. Grandpa believed in doing things the natural way; he didn't use store-bought medicine. After he took two pieces of rock salt out of my left cheek, he applied lots of lemon juice. I can't tell you how that felt! Grandpa didn't say much about the incident; he just asked why I hadn't taken one of *his* watermelons. He didn't seem to understand that the other tasted much better.

After we boys healed, we decided that Farmer Ferdinand's action could not go unpunished. We drew up our plan, and the next evening, we went into action. Sneaking onto his property, we quietly removed the outhouse and carried it to the end of his property.

Using our skill—plus our blocks and tackles—we lifted the outhouse to the top of the barn and got it to stay there. The whole operation only took two hours. Then we fled as fast as we could.

Then, laughing and feeling on top of the world, we went our separate ways. I would've loved to have seen old Farmer Ferdinand's face when he couldn't find his outhouse.

The following morning, the sheriff came up to see Grandpa. They talked awhile, then called me over. They asked if I knew anything about Farmer Ferdinand and his outhouse. I assured them I had no knowledge of anything that happened on that man's property.

Grandpa sent me on my way to do my chores, and that was the end of that. Later that day, however, Grandpa took his tractor with the big iron wheels over to Farmer Ferdinand's, and they removed the outhouse from the barn and put it back in place.

Now, had I been a suspicious person, I would have thought Grandpa knew exactly what had happened, because from that moment on, my wonderful summer vacation turned into a nightmare. Grandpa had me bring items to Farmer Ferdinand almost every day. (I'd never had to do that before.) I carried bushel baskets to him in the wheelbarrow. I made four trips that day—and it was a mile walk.

Other days, I carried tools, barbed wire, fencing material—you get the idea. Of course, these items had to be brought back home, too. Even my chores increased. Why, I

didn't get to see Basil and Robbie at all. The remaining five weeks of summer felt like prison.

Mind you, Grandpa never said anything to me about the incident. But he did say funny things to Nana at supper, like "Hard work is good for the soul," and "While working, a person gets to do a lot of thinking," and "If you are doing hard work, it should be worthwhile and not for some silly reason."

Finally, the summer drew to an end. I was more than happy to get back to the city and school. The day I left was one of the most enlightening days in my life. As he did every year, Grandpa hugged me and told me how helpful I had been on the farm. He told me he couldn't have gotten all the chores done without me. He also gave me some of the money he had saved from selling the vegetables. He always told me to put some away and use some for the movies.

Just before Dad pulled out of the drive, Grandpa said one more thing to me in a very low voice. He told me that the sheriff had returned one of his pulleys the day he dropped by after the outhouse caper. Seems it was found by Farmer Ferdinand's barn. Grandpa was in the habit of burning his initials into all his tools and equipment. He said it stopped any argument about who owned an item. It also made it easy to return if it was left somewhere.

Grandpa was a lot smarter than I gave him credit for. Needless to say, that summer was a lesson well taught. I learned the value of being honest and working hard for good things, not bad. But it just seems to me that Grandpa had a little too much fun teaching me that lesson during that long, long summer.

Thanks, Grandpa! ❖

—Originally published in July 1999.

Good Old Days magazine cover, June 1998, © *Down by the Creek* by Jim Daly

A Lesson Learned

By Birney Dibble

I was sick and tired of being called a sissy because I rode a girl's bike to deliver my newspapers! My sister, Elsie, was two years older than I and had been given a bike by a young couple whose daughter had died. She "rented" the bike to me for 10 cents a week, provided I used it only for my "work."

I often settled my weekly debt by paying her way to the Tuesday-night movie, which was 10-Cent Night. (Of course, I wouldn't be caught dead sitting with her; no red-blooded, 10-year-old American boy would.)

It was 1935, so I probably don't have to explain why my parents didn't just go out and buy me a boy's bike. My father was a Methodist minister making $100 a month—enough to live on, but not enough to buy a bicycle.

I picked up my papers on the back loading dock of a hardware store run by my pal Bob's father, Fred Harris. In the front window of the store was a beautiful red bike. It had everything: balloon tires, fenders, brakes, chain guard, a ding-a-ling horn on the handlebars, a wire basket behind the adjustable seat and, incredibly, a battery case between the two transverse bars to power a real headlight. Wow!

But it was priced out of reach—$32, which I thought was exorbitant. It was more than my father made in a week.

One day I was sitting on my sister's bike in front of the store, canvas sack for my papers hanging on my shoulder, gazing longingly at that bike in the window. Mr. Harris came out to wash his windows and saw me sitting there.

"Got your eye on that bike, Birney?" he said.

"Yes, sir."

"How much do you make a week delivering those papers?"

"Four dollars and 50 cents, if everyone pays." Which they often didn't, of course, because they couldn't always come up with the weekly 15 cents.

I wondered why he asked. I soon found out. "Could you come up with a dollar a week, do you think, if I sold you that bike?"

I was stunned. I didn't know that you could pay for things a little bit at a time. My parents never did, except maybe for big things like a car. And I wasn't sure they would let me do such a thing. "Well," I said finally, "I sure think I could, if my dad would let me."

"Go ask him."

I delivered those 30 papers faster than ever before and raced home. I could tell that my father didn't think much of the idea. But my mother put her hand on his shoulder and said, "Let him do it."

He looked up at her and then back at me. "All right," he said.

So I ran downtown—it was only three blocks—and told Mr. Harris I had come for "my" bike.

I handed him a dollar and, with emotions that I didn't understand at the time, I rode that bike all over town. One emotion that I identified later was guilt for being so happy when the bike really wasn't mine yet. But for the next 31 weeks, the very first thing I did every Saturday morning after making my collections was pedal down to Mr. Harris' hardware store to proudly hand him a dollar bill. Then I watched him write in his accounts book, and he gave me a receipt.

Mr. Harris did an uncommonly grand thing for me that day. He put his *trust* in me, a 10-year-old kid with no assets except himself. I wasn't old enough to fully appreciate that then, but even so, it was a lesson in living that I've never forgotten. It was many years later before I realized that he hadn't even charged me interest.

I kept that bike until I joined the Navy eight years later, in 1943. Then I gave it to a young cousin, who, of all things, needed it to deliver his papers. That's the way things were done in the Good Old Days. ❖

—Originally published in September 1999.